D0788966

THE POWER
OF
INDIGNATION

THE POWER OF INDIGNATION

THE AUTOBIOGRAPHY OF THE MAN WHO INSPIRED THE
ARAB SPRING

STÉPHANE HESSEL

TRANSLATION BY E. C. BELLI

Skyhorse Publishing

Skyhorse Publishing books may be purchased in bulk at special discounts for sales promotion, corporate gifts, fund-raising, or educational purposes. Special editions can also be created to specifications. For details, contact the Special Sales Department, Skyhorse Publishing, 307 West 36th Street, 11th Floor, New York, NY 10018 or info@skyhorsepublishing.com.

Skyhorse® and Skyhorse Publishing® are registered trademarks of Skyhorse Publishing, Inc.®, a Delaware corporation.

Visit our website at www.skyhorsepublishing.com.

10 9 8 7 6 5 4 3 2 1

Library of Congress Cataloging-in-Publication Data is available on file.

ISBN: 978-1-62087-092-1

Printed in the United States of America

Table of Contents

Editor's Note

Stéphane Hessel's words reach beyond the boundaries of a mere book. His is a cry meant to open our eyes and activate our consciences. Accordingly, this volume is not an autobiography in the traditional sense of the term, i.e. one that is backward looking. It is, instead, an invitation to courage. In these pages you will find experiences that have proven valuable by inciting within Hessel a certain political engagement and a certain outlook on life.

The editor would like to thank all of those who, through their stimulating presence, came to occupy a place in this book. Thanks also to Sacha Goldman of the International Ethical, Scientific and Political Collegium, an indefatigable leader of an organization where intelligence and experience meet in the aim of conceiving of wiser forms of governance for both humanity and the planet as a whole.

M. S.

Author's Introduction

This is the tale of an entire life, a tale marked by chance encounters, by blossoming and withering relationships, by memories revisited and experienced now as though through a glass thickening in the dimming light of evening: "Again you show yourselves, you wavering Forms, / Revealed, as you once were, to clouded vision…"

Contained within these pages is an entire set of principles, of values, and of ethics too, erected from unshakable bases: Walter Benjamin, Hannah Arendt, Merleau-Ponty, and all of the great artists and writers of the past. Special mention to Edgar Morin, Régis Debray, Michel Rocard, Daniel Cohn-Bendit, Jean-Claude Carrière, Peter Sloterdijk, Laure Adler, Jean-Paul Dollé, and so many others from the present. To yet another *Danse avec le siècle*[1] that now begins.

---

[1] In 1997, Stéphane Hessel published an autobiography titled *Danse avec le Siècle (Dance with the Century)*.

Dedication[2]

Again you show yourselves, you wavering Forms,
Revealed, as you once were, to clouded vision.
Shall I attempt to hold you fast once more?
Heart's willing still to suffer that illusion?
You crowd so near! Well then, you shall endure,
And rouse me, from your mist and cloud's confusion:
My spirit feels so young again: it's shaken
By magic breezes that your breathings awaken.

You bring with you the sight of joyful days,
And many a loved shade rises to the eye:
And like some other half-forgotten phrase,
First Love returns, and Friendship too is nigh:
Pain is renewed, and sorrow: all the ways,
Life wanders in its labyrinthine flight,
Naming the good, those that Fate has robbed
Of lovely hours, those slipped from me and lost.

---

[2] Kline, A.S. "Goethe, Faust - Part I Prologue - A New English Translation." *Poetry In Translation*. Web. 09 Mar. 2012. <http://www.poetryintranslation.com/PITBR/German/FaustIProl.htm>.

One

The Gift of Years

"Gleich der Flamme:" like a flame…

I had already begun what I believed was the final chapter in the large book I like to call "My Life"—eight lovely and equally beloved decades marked by myriad adventures of love and of the mind, when an unexpected, inconceivable, and yet irrepressible set of circumstances transformed the life of this old, retired diplomat into a circus. A short text with a provocative title[3] that had flowed from my pen took off like a rocket, crossing at once all borders, and has now incited innumerable readers to outrage. I hadn't considered the kind of risk I was taking or the sometimes fervent response with which this cry from the heart would be met. What I had unleashed

---

[3] Hessel is referring to *Time for Outrage.*

was a hurricane. I needed to understand the reasons behind this response and, above all, evaluate the consequences. Yes, this pamphlet came at the right time. Our global society, held under the yoke of various financial pressures for the past twenty years (a trend in the face of which individual governments found themselves unable to protect their own citizens), seemed gloomy and incoherent. A summons of sorts, which called upon the values of freedom and justice that my own generation had looked to in its efforts to build a better world after the horrendous tumult of the '40s (first by opposing the way in which those values had been trampled both by North African tyrants and by some imperfect democracies amongst our own developed nations), this call to outrage certainly came at the right time. But I couldn't leave it at that. The door, now opened, had to lead somewhere. I had to give substance to this message that those born during World War I felt, in their hearts, must be shared with the new generation facing new threats on the cusp of the twenty-first century.

Besides my surprise at having struck the right chord merely by scribbling onto paper a few simple ideas that were, in my mind, obvious facts, the whole affair provided me great joy. A true *joie de vivre* rekindled within me, and lasts even to this day, each time an audience full of young spectators comes to me with anxious questions—questions that I unavoidably end up answering with poems. This quiet old ambassador has such high expectations placed upon him (expectations which he alone is responsible for creating). It's always a moment amidst the stars.

So there I was, having traveled to all corners of Europe—Warsaw, Düsseldorf, Madrid, Turin, Milan, Lisbon—promoting a rather violent message, a message of outrage that, in sum, declared: Refuse the unacceptable. I suppose this could have inspired some fear within me that I had gone too far perhaps, or that I could no longer live up to expectations. Yet, quite the opposite, this moment has become, in the old age that is now mine (ninety-four in 2011!), emblematic of a last-minute resurgence, and has offered me a new window on the world and on my contemporaries.

But does the life I have lived entitle me to all of this? That is the question underlying this book. What is it about this long life of mine that allows me to carry forth such a message? What do I know of men, of women, and of love? What do I know of science, of philosophy, of politics? What could I possibly have to say about the magical encounters that mark our lives and gave me a taste for wonder? And what did I learn from them? What do I owe my family, my childhood, and my sentimental education? Does having been instilled, as a child, with a love for poetry have some impact today on my relationships, on my interlocutors, and on my audiences who are as young as they are attentive to the words of this old man?

And while we're at it, has the fact that I have learned three different languages over the course of my life, languages, which each delight me in equal measure and in their own way, made expression of feeling and communication somewhat easier for me? I believe so—yet, what a disappointment to not be able to speak Spanish, or Russian, or other similarly-seductive languages!

"Let us turn to the past: that will be progress"

This quote by Giuseppe Verdi, whispered into my ninety-year-old ear by Régis Debray, resonates well. I appreciate the fact that my words carry weight merely because they result from a long life in which I have known, encountered, and discovered many things—a life filled with myriad adventures. But the collected memories of a human being do constitute a treasure of insights. What lends legitimacy to my words is precisely the fact that I have crossed a century full of inventions, hopes, and horrors, and that I have fully participated in that adventure. I think I perhaps owe my life a debt of insight and maybe that debt can be repaid today by sharing this account. Caught somewhere between l'éclipse de la durée, the disintegration of generational bonds, and *The Society of the Spectacle,*[4] the implications of old age in our modern era are peculiar. Past experiences sometimes seem less important in the eyes of my contemporaries than those future experiences, those experiences yet to be had. In his little *Essai d'intoxication volontaire,*[5] Peter Sloterdijk speaks of an "integral disinheritance," which he defines as, "This strange way in which younger generations separate from their parents in a single jolt" (even if it means having to relearn everything on their own). The questions arise: What could an old chap like me have to offer the world, and why

---

[4]   Guy Debord's critical work which posits that modern society's authentic social life has been replaced with its representation: "All that was once directly lived has become mere representation."

[5]   Sloterdijk, Peter. *Essai D'intoxication Volontaire: Conversation Avec Carlos Oliveira.* Paris: Calmann-Lévy, 1999. Print.

should attention be paid to me instead of another? After all, I don't really have the philosophical training required to be a thinker in matters of politics. Once again, it is *experience* rather than an ability to engage in theoretical thinking that gives these words value.

The time has perhaps come for me to consider all that I have said and done. Many times over the course of the past few years I have thought of doing so and considered it, in fact, for the very first time in 1996. I was seventy-nine at the time and the publisher Editions du Seuil had asked me to recount my life. But I've never really considered myself a writer, though I did come to know of that peculiar way of being and living during my childhood, through my father. Indeed, he devoted his entire life to writing and almost held himself apart from anything that was not literary; an admirable fate, but not an enviable one. No, in my own life, I wanted to be immersed in the current of the world. Consequently, I hesitated quite a bit before taking pen to page. It was only upon Françoise Peyrot's insistence (then Director of Collections[6] at Editions du Seuil) that I accepted. That experience of taking stock of it all was, for me, looking back at the first eighty years of my life as though they had been a dance through the century—a century that is ending now, at the same time as my own existence on this earth, and a dance, that cannot yet clearly be called macabre or merry, that might either mark, in the long history of human society, a dusk or a dawn.

---

[6]   The English equivalent of an editorial director.

Eight years later I took stock of it all for a second time in a way that was particularly close to my heart. I was going to be eighty-eight years old, a number that fascinates me. If you lay them down horizontally, those two eights become two symbols of infinity—infinite like the field of energy that is created by the eighty-eight poems I know by heart and enjoy reciting.

My relationship with Laure Adler, who, at the time, suddenly became head of the Editions du Seuil and decided to publish *O Ma Mémoire,*[7] is a very *poetry-based* relationship. Accordingly, I chose to examine the connection between man and poetry in that volume, which ended up being a trilingual anthology of more than thirty French poems, approximately twenty German poems, and another twenty in English. By then the end of my life had drawn yet closer and had taken for me the welcome form that Rainer Maria Rilke evokes when describing us as bees that "madly gather the honey of the visible in order to accumulate it in the grand golden hive of the Invisible."[8] But the end did not come. Still alert, I crossed the threshold of ninety and became a survivor, one of those increasingly rare survivors of a memory that has suddenly become essential and whose full significance needs to be explored once again. Before long, I found myself at the Glières Plateau with a message for the generations that follow me: "Resisting is creating. Creating is resisting."

Isn't "all said and done" the truest motto to ever suit me? It's a motto I actually used to close off my interviews

---

7   Hessel, Stéphane. *O Ma Mémoire: La Poésie, Ma Nécessité.* Paris: Seuil, 2006. Print.

8   Rilke, Rainer Maria. *The Duino Elegies.* Trans. Leslie Norris and Alan Frank Keele. Rochester: Camden House, 2008. Print.

with Jean-Michel Helvig in *Citoyen sans frontières*[9]—a book of mine that ends with "The Pretty Redhead," the poem by Guillaume Apollinaire whose own final line closes humbly: "Have pity on me."

But had all been said and done yet? No. A woman, who was amongst the three thousand people who came to this exceptional place, to this superb Savoyard landscape where the moving memory of our lost comrades lives on, heard me. After hearing me proclaim the important role of those old values which must not be forgotten or desecrated (as they are by too many governments, like our own) at every stage in our history, Sylvie Crossman, co-director, with Jean-Pierre Barou, of Indigene Editions, resolved to make me work some more. A few months later, *Time For Outrage*, that little libel whose unbelievable reach opened a new chapter in my life, was born from our meetings. There was, after all, still something left for me to do.

Today, it is once again a woman, Maren Sell, the editor who worked on the French translations of my father Franz Hessel's books some twenty-five years ago, who invited me to put together some sort of treatise for younger generations on the ways in which one might go about leading the life of an activist. Her request came in the spring of 2010, a few months before I became a media darling. This present attempt at taking stock of my life and of what meaning to give to it, I shan't dare wish that it might actually be the last.

---

[9]   Hessel, Stéphane. *Citoyen Sans Frontières: Conversations Avec Jean-Michel Helvig.* Paris: Fayard, 2008. Print.

Ecce Homo[10]

Yes! I know from where I came!
Ever hungry like a flame
I consume myself and glow.
Light grows all that I conceive,
ashes everything I leave:
Flame I am assuredly.

---

[10] Nietzsche, Friedrich, and Walter Kaufmann. *The Gay Science: With a Prelude in Rhymes and an Appendix of Songs : Translated, with Commentary by Walter Kaufmann.* New York: Random, 1974. Print.

Two

Refusing the Unacceptable

All human beings are born free and equal in dignity and rights…

So what is it exactly that I have learned and must convey? First, that it is necessary and possible to refuse the unacceptable. Throughout the decades, men who have resigned themselves, who gave up, who considered their fight lost and estimated that nothing could be done—whether they were dissenters unable to unify fully before taking power or whether they became non-resistant after the victory of murderous powers—well, something has eluded those men forever, something which is supposed to distinguish man in his dignity.

In 1948, when those who drafted the Universal Declaration of Human Rights attempted to characterize a human person, the term they deemed fitting to all religions, to all philosophies, and which they finally selected was, indeed, *dignity*. It is also the concept which inspires the first article of the said Declaration and which sums up, in my eyes, the entire predicament in which our contemporary world finds itself: "All human beings are born free and equal in dignity and rights. They are endowed with reason and conscience and should act towards one another in a spirit of brotherhood." The unacceptable is infringement upon another's dignity. This infringement can sometimes cleverly pose as the rejection of another because this other is *justifiably* deemed to be missing something, because he is 'too other,' too incapable or lacking. I say no one can ever be *justifiably* treated as inferior. Such a treatment is unacceptable. What is justified, however, is to be outraged at such a treatment. This is also the situation in which outrage must find its true path and result in actual engagement. For, were outrage to merely remain in this formless state of antagonism and were it to wither and turn to anger, nothing would come of it but some gnashing of teeth. Nevertheless, determining what deserves our outrage is the first skill I owe myself to teach those who are going to be protesting this new world and the grave dangers we face. It all boils down to having a conscience.

"The starry sky above me and the moral law within me," or impulse and the law

This need for us to have a conscience is a complex idea, for a conscience needs to be developed, cultivated, and maintained.

Unless you expect to be visited by the Holy Spirit and instructed on the various forms of eternal grace on your way to Damascus, Jerusalem, Benares, or Lhasa (a scenario that lacks both likelihood and courage), I believe we must commit to giving ourselves the means to make our consciences emerge. What we need is an education in the ways of developing a conscience. What we need is an at-once-gentle-and-yet-strict apprenticeship that takes into consideration the dialectic presented by impulse vs. the law, of dream vs. reality, of "human rights" and of "another's rights," a dialectic that considers all of these things and their respective limits and constraints; limits and constraints we must both learn to recognize and to resist.

One day, Jean-Claude Carrière pointed out to me to what extent it was illusory to him, and all in all dangerous, to have faith in the essential goodness of human nature. He claims that Rousseau's 'myth' would have us believe that, were men and women to act as they wish, everything would go well in the world and all sources of moral corruption (meaning the power structures in place) would be eliminated. He is, of course, right to emphasize that such a scenario is implausible. In all present cultures token gestures of liberty (the carrot) and the stick must be combined in order to help preserve actual liberty. We know full well that we are not made only of good intentions. We know full well that if we were left to act on our own, we wouldn't necessarily take the path of fairness, balance, generosity, and of all those noble notions we always like to hold forth. It is such an admission that requires us to seek to impose a law upon ourselves; for indeed, we must consent to law.

But the law only draws its power from the sources out of which it is born, from the values it looks to defend and from the injustices against which it must protect us. We must always be able to find justification at its root, for when that is absent, the law should no longer earn the support of those she claims to cast her reach over. The refusal to obey, which was exhibited recently by some of our teachers, for instance, is, in that respect, completely justifiable. Additionally, the fact that a government is elected through a democratic process is not sufficient to ensure that all of its decisions will be informed by a clear knowledge of what is right and what cannot be.

This reminds me of Walter Benjamin's eloquence in presenting his hypotheses on the philosophy of history: in our quest for progress, it is important to focus our efforts primarily on those who are most marginalized, least respected, and the most destitute members of the population. This word, *progress*, is not suited to define the current process of endless accumulation of resources that is enjoyed by dominant oligarchies, whose vigorous breath causes Paul Klee's angel with spread wings to withdraw, terrorized, in his *Angelus Novus*—an image Benjamin was never able to let go of.

We instinctively address our reproaches to tyrants, and we sing the praises of those who make them fall. It is not as easy, though it is just as necessary, to address with enough energy and make heard our criticism of modern democracies, which have shown themselves insensitive to the most basic needs of the true victims of the law, which, we have come to find, seeks to protect the property of the privileged first and foremost.

At once, the importance of having representatives selected directly from amongst the people, as were the carriers of the *cahiers de doléances*[11] during the assembly of constituents of 1789, asserts itself. The role of those representatives is especially significant during moments of historic progress in our societies. Today, the carriers of the *cahiers d'espérance,*[12] called upon by Claude Alphandéry to extend the reach of the Social and United Economy,[13] represent real solutions to the unbearable tyranny of the market. During the foreign occupation of a broken France, the members of the National Council of the Resistance (NCR), brought together by Jean Moulin to draft the program[14] that I once again defended at the Plateau de Glières because its values are so threatened today, were similarly significant.

---

[11] Registers of grievances presented by the people to King Louis XVI in 1789, in which each Estate (the clergy, the nobility, and the bourgeois, peasants, and workers) were given the opportunity to express their hopes and complaints directly to the monarch.

[12] Registers of hope (the name alludes to the registers of grievances of 1789) in which activist and militant members of the new Economie Sociale et Solidaire (ESS) movement, or Social and United Economy, expressed their ideas for a new, more just economy during the ESS's convention in Lille, France in June 2011. The convention was held at the initiative of Claude Alphandéry, a former French Resistant, banker, economist, and President of the IAE (Insertion par l'Activité Economique), an organization founded in the 1970s which looks to hire individuals who have been unemployed for a long period of time and is one of the organizations that constitutes the ESS movement.

[13] The Social and United Economy, or Economie Sociale et Solidaire (ESS), is a recent movement whose stated goal is to encourage engagement on behalf its members in launching a plea for a more just economy that would consider man and the environment above all in its doings. More information: www. pouruneautreeconomie.fr.

[14] Hessel is referring to the program drafted by the NCR, which suggested plans for a social democracy and planned economy after the liberation. The program was adopted shortly before Jean Moulin's death and today some parts of that program are actually in use in France.

Those Resistants and Resistantes had no other mandate than a task to accomplish; a task addressed to all, regardless of their hierarchical position; a task issued from their convictions alone. And finally, in the years that followed, under the Third Reich—a time in which the most abominable of modern killings were taking place—the members of the Commission who were chosen, based on competence alone and not designated by their respective governments, to draft the Universal Declaration of Human Rights: were they, too, of incredible worth?

That's it for men, but what about the planet? At the time of the Universal Declaration of Human Rights, we were not conscious that our responsibilities would involve anything beyond the way in which human societies act toward each other. Perhaps we were still too focused on those disappointing, characteristic concepts of the Judeo-Christian tradition, which conceives of man as being created by God, the master of Creation, and not as part of a larger whole. Evidently, the risk of excess was considerable.

Jean-Claude Carrière sometimes attributes man's exploitation of nature to the words found in Genesis. It is possible that, in our Western traditions, there still lingers in us a sense of supremacy over nature that is very different from what we find in the religions of Asia. The church did try, at some point, to make up for the consequences of this Promethean hubris. But, on the one hand, its influence has considerably waned, and on the other, it is difficult to move past. You might remember the words preached in the nineteenth century in Pope Pius IX's encyclical *Syllabus of Errors*: Everything that comes from new ideas must be rejected; we must hold fast to the ancient texts. It's truly alarming. And 1864 was not that long ago.

But those are established views *par excellence.*[15] Were we to strictly stick to biblical texts, we would be lost, for we cannot usurp the earth without destroying ourselves too in the process. We need to accept this idea: one need not be a Buddhist to recognize that the Earth *is* Man and vice-versa. Milan Kučan, president of Slovenia, likes to share this quote attributed to Karl Marx: "In the conflict between Nature and Man, we know who is at fault."

The Scientist, the Businessman, and the Politician

Refusing the unacceptable is only the first step. What must follow is the indispensable evolution of mindsets toward a true collective conscience fostered by creative thought. I must say that it is impressive how—by entertaining a close intellectual relationship with thinkers from back in the day, such as Benjamin, Adorno, Sartre, or Merleau-Ponty, or thinkers of today, such as Sloterdijk, Carrière, Debraz, or Morin (and I am not even mentioning them all)—many diverse scientific, political, and poetic minds can all converge into a single plea for an increased awareness of our problems and a refocusing on what really matters.

I will concede that in certain circles it may appear that voting preferences are preset. Yet, the idea that humanity, at the very least as far as its Western subdivision is concerned, is

---

[15]   French expression that means "by definition." Used for emphasis.

on the brink of making significant moral and scientific strides just cannot be shaken from me and is quite my own. The moral and political crises in which we are currently engaged are not unrelated. Only fear of the unknown, apprehension toward change, reticence to embrace "an occurrence happening in man" (to use Heidegger's words), still keeps us in too conservative and nervous a state of denial.

Let us reflect for a moment on the state of science. What has most progressed over the course of the past twenty or thirty years is science. It has made *fantastic* progress. We now have much more detailed information on human beings, the world, and matter. And yet, the scientist is not a type known only to inspire great esteem. He is known, in fact, for prioritizing first and foremost the pleasure derived from the success of his invention or of his discovery, without necessarily pondering its consequent dangers. He is akin to a child playing with marbles, which turn out to be bombs. As Sloterdijk reminds us, whether we want it or not, we are today the guardians of nuclear fire and of the genetic code. When we think of our relationship to science and technology, we must take into consideration the fact that we hold a type of knowledge that has turned us into improbable demiurges. The chief example is the atom bomb, which is not a scientific problem, but rather a matter of politics: yesterday, Hiroshima; then, Chernobyl; and finally, Fukushima. These are serious problems facing humanity, as are stem cell research, biogenetics, cloning, GMOs, and so on.

If it all goes too far, we must refuse the unacceptable, and it is that form of conscience that the politician has been charged to embody and defend. As regards nuclear energy, the question is not whether it is possible to know, both scientifically and technologically speaking, if it can be achieved with zero risk. No, the question is whether a community is prepared to collectively assume the consequences posed by nuclear power. And those types of questions should fall, by virtue of his responsibilities, to the politician. The scientist need not step into the shoes of the politician and the politician need not resign when in the scientist's presence; especially when the businessman has invited himself into this relationship and is trying hard to plot them against each other in hopes of making a substantial profit.

What is the role of science today? And what is the role it is encouraged to play in the interest of profit? Here is an indispensable question, a question to which I obviously don't have a definitive answer. I am tempted to refer back to that famous quote, "Science without conscience…"[16] It is not so much science itself that is alienating, but the *scientification* of everything that surrounds us. Science is dangerous because it tends to ignore the needs of others in its attempt at self-realization. For a few years already, I have been wary of this term *science*, especially when science is conjectured to be the wise guide that it actually isn't. Too often we are quick to abandon our common sense and blindly follow scientifically-proven solutions, sidestepping

---

[16]   Full quote is issued from François Rabelais' *Pantagruel* (1532): "But as the wise Solomon said, wisdom enters not into a malicious mind, and science without conscience is but the ruin of the soul, thus it behooves you to serve, to love, to fear God, and on him to repose all your thoughts and all your hope, and by faith formed in charity to adhere to him, so that you may never be separated from him by your sins."

necessary reflection on the world and all of its complexities in the process. Then too, things must be scientifically proven or we do not believe them to exist. But what about the *homo ludens,*[17] the *homo demens*[18] that Edgar Morin speaks of in his *Method?*[19] What about all of those things that do not fall strictly within the scope of science? Above all, what about our imagination and our ability to conjure up a world that would make use of all of those discoveries? What I hear being said about nanotechnology, for instance, worries me. It's as if the type of reductive thinking that has been at play in finance for the past thirty years unfortunately continues to live on in this new form of scientism that claims, "We have all the answers. Governments have best leave us be. Everything will work like clockwork." Granted, of course, that they get to keep the clock!

I lament the absence of public debate on the motivations behind certain funding decisions and the ways in which our scientific discoveries are put to use. I recognize in this Marx's notions of historical materialism and scientific socialism, Augustus Comte's technocratic doctrines,[20] and of course the oppressive nature of the market, always eager to broaden its scope, to which only the living represent a barrier.

---

[17]   "The man of play"; a concept put forth in Morin's *Method*.

[18]   "The man of dementia"; a concept put forth in Morin's *Method*.

[19]   Edgar Morin's 5-volume work, *La Méthode*, has limited availability in English. Only Volume 1 has been translated and it is currently out of print: Morin, Edgar. *Method: Towards a Study of Humankind.* Trans. J.L. Roland Bélanger. Vol. 1. New York U.a.: Lang, 1992. Print.

[20]   Augustus Comte (1798-1857) is at the origin of French Positivism. One of his ideas was to replace the Catholic clergy with a new elite: technocrats.

Never has the tension between facts and morals been as heavy with consequences as in our contemporary world. Each in their own way, Edgar Morin and Peter Sloterdijk both remind us that science has become a formidable force today, but a force that has evaded any sort of ethical regulations, and also that politically motivated regulation ranges from stupidly prohibitive to blindly permissive.

There is another limit to science, a more poetic one this time, as highlighted in Morin's books. Thanks to science, we have discovered astonishing things concerning the universe, reality, and life; but all of this marvelous knowledge actually leads to yet a deeper mystery. We know the universe came about as the result of some sort of explosion, but from whence, out of which abyss? We do not know. What truth do we find behind this truth by examining reality through the lens of microphysics? To where does dissolved matter vanish? What is the origin of the universe, its limits? Why did life emerge? Why does man *exist*? There are so many mysteries. But unexplainable does not necessarily mean impossible.

In his books, and in particular in his *Method*, Morin presents a rich and original view of the brain's future. In a multi-pronged approach that considers brain studies, cybernetics, and information theory, Morin underlines a fascinating convergence of different approaches to our understanding of the functioning of the machines inside our skulls. It is a mistake, according to him, to believe that the scope of research can be limited to a single subject or field. We must understand this paradox: our mind expresses itself through words; but our neurons express themselves through electrochemical exchanges. There is, as a result, quite an intricate relationship between the language of the brain and the language of the mind. It is wrong, however, to reduce the scope of the mind merely to that of the brain.

What we should remark, however, is that, within a given cultural environment, the human brain makes it possible for a mind to arise, a mind which can speak and express feelings. Take as proof the many cases of children-wolves or abandoned children who are found living like primates due to their isolation from society and lack of interaction with their peers. Their inability to speak proves that it is out of contact with a certain culture, a certain language, and certain set of knowledge, and also because of the way in which those interactions influence our brains, that a mind can emerge. Culture is a cocoon, a womb, a fertile space where this 'program' can grow.

Like Morin, we should bemoan the fact that the different branches of contemporary neurosciences have not yet succeeded in coordinating their efforts and remain relatively separate, in the same way other sciences do; which, of course, does not make their research any easier. But we do know some fascinating things already. For instance, the brain scans of Buddhist monks in a fully meditative state have revealed much about the brain's function during this rather ascetic practice; the brain structures supposed to distinguish between the self and the non-self cease to function. It's fascinating. A comparable effect occurs during sexual climax, in which individuals are found to reach fulfillment and lose control all at once. Such is the first lesson in human complexity.

This lesson from the scientist is addressed to the politician. Let's hope he will learn it before the businessman does!

Solving the deadlock: considering life in all of its parts

When the businessman rules, cold, hard mathematics rule. We will have to prove our ability to separate ourselves from that. For it is impossible to consider a human being in all of his or her parts if we limit ourselves to mere numbers. There are thousands of ways in which to objectively take measure of a human being, such as through electroencephalograms, body measurements, and psychoanalysis, to name a few. But in truth, reality eschews numbers. Life, death, morals, love, and hate all eschew the "reign of quantity."[21]

Herein lies the superiority of art, whether we are speaking of poetry and its transgressive nature, theater and its cathartic representation of reality, film and its oneiric dramatizations of our imagination, or novels, which blend all of the categories cited above. The novel goes deeper yet than the social sciences, deeper than psychology or sociology. It portrays concrete beings in all of their subjectivity and in all of their diverse environments. It was Ernesto Sabato who said in sum that, nowadays, the only laboratory in which we can examine the complete spectrum of human conditions is in fiction.

It also seems to me that poetry (more so than science) is able to reveal what is deepest and most essential in all of us,

---

[21] Hessel may be alluding to *Le Règne de la Quantité et les Signes des Temps*, a book by René Guénon (Gallimard, 1945). Also available in English : Guénon, René. *The Reign of Quantity & the Signs of the times*. Trans. Lord Northbourne. Ed. James R. Wetmore. Ghent, NY: Sophia Perennis, 2001. Print.

this heartbeat that contains the world and that is shared by all human beings. Let us therefore listen to the advice of a wise man like Morin. Let us recognize the limitations of scientific truths and their shortcomings. Even scientists, who are able to consider everything they look at objectively, are incapable of recognizing their own subjectivity, of truly knowing themselves. This is what Husserl suggested at a wonderful conference in 1930, by claiming that there was a black hole in the brains of scientists: "They do not know who they are. They know things, but they do not know what they are doing."

Let us not forget that science is a wonderfully human adventure whose destination still remains unknown. Choosing its final destination is not the sole purview of the scientist. It must include the poet, the politician, the citizen, the moralist, and the philosopher.

In a very moving anti-Cartesian impulse, Merleau-Ponty admitted at the ENS[22] that a human being is an indissociable compound of body and soul. It is a poignant idea that has remained dear to me and allows me to live out my relationships with others more fully, whether they are loved ones or mere acquaintances. I am sensitive both to exchanges based on intellect and to emotion, to what warms the heart and to what makes us think.

Merleau-Ponty was a great philosopher whose main quality was that he emphasized what he referred to as the "flesh." Too many thinkers believe that the conceptual nature of their ideas somehow lends gravity to their thoughts. But

---

[22]   École Normale Supérieure in Paris

they forget reality—the body. Kierkegaard, deriding Hegelian philosophy, quipped, "The Herr Professor knows everything that exists in the world, but he no longer knows what he himself is." And yet, warnings against this tendency toward taking a theoretical view of beings and of their being-in-the-world is already addressed to us as early as Socrates.

Manifestly, philosophy could cause its own degeneration, were it to retreat completely into the barren territories of theorization and become impervious to the soul's pulsations. I think that nowadays, in our *art de vivre,*[23] we cannot merely aspire, as we once did, to being wise—since it has indeed been proven that we have great potential for folly in us. Let's admit it. A completely reasonable life is neither possible, nor desirable. The essence of existence lies in a necessary combination of reason and passion. In other words, passion cannot exist without reason and reason cannot exist without passion.

As for the degeneration of philosophy, it is well summed up by a perfidious and impertinent phrase by Sloterdijk: "We find contemporary philosophy at its best nowadays when we witness it in its attempts at justifying how it would posit a given problem if it actually had something to contribute." Harsh, but true. And yet, its contributions are doubly needed. On the one hand, philosophy provides us with the means to call into question things that have, up until then, seemed like immovable truths. On the other hand, it seeks to establish a certain correspondence between our actual lives and the life

---

[23]   "Way of life"

of the mind. Achieving such a unity would amount to living our human lives to the fullest and would act as a safeguard against cynics, for this type of unity would prove the good sense of this honest humanist.

What seeks the light of day

Refusing the inacceptable is, obviously, refusing the world as it is. Albert Camus once said, "If there was something to conserve in this world, I would be a conservative." Evidently, certain of our accomplishments are precious and it is unacceptable to question them.

So we must call upon our creative potential as humans. What good is it to claim that we are rebuilding the world when we are in fact throwing out ready-made theories, which we hope others will read, others whom we hope will suddenly become enlightened upon learning about our great plans? The true challenge, today, is to help deliver a concrete version of this new world of tomorrow, to help bring about what seeks the light of day. Everywhere this rise in awareness is taking place, human resourcefulness is in action. There are co-ops, mutually supportive, more-or-less self-directed interest groups, which thrive through unity with nature, organic farming, etc. Those groups are alive; but they are isolated and ignored by administrations, by political parties, and by the dominant structures. All of these citizen-led movements remain in the margins, or are not strong enough yet to resist attempts at assimilation, normalization, or regularization; which all result from a capitalist mindset. The real challenge is to make those examples known, recognized, and shared, so that they may synergize and feed a wider move-ment of reforms. Like Edgar Morin, I believe that, in the end, everything must be reformed. Not only the ossified, bureau-cratized administrations and institutions, and not only the economy, the markets, and distribution; but *everything*, includ-ing nutrition and consumerism. It's our entire lives we must change. All of these reforms, including educational reform and the reform of mindsets, are interconnected, interdependent—each must enter a juggling act to avoid both losing momentum and becoming isolated from the others. The ex-USSR proved it. Completely changing the economy, in the end, does not change habits, human beings, anything at all. On the contrary, the result is simply the founding of new dictatorships.

The idea is therefore to contribute to the transformation of our existence, to create multiple pathways which would merge into a single way that would lead us toward metamorphosis.

Such are the premises of the politics of hope. Believ-ing that nothing can be accomplished without hope, I had, during the European elections of 2009, signed a vibrant plea, alongside Peter Sloterdijk and Paul Virilio, that called upon the infinite resources issued from creativity and hope: "Europe écologie : pour une politique de l'espérance."[24]

Sadly, it would seem that most seniors have lost hope, perhaps from having been wrong so many times through-out history. As for young people, they don't seem to really know where to look to anymore from being so direction-

---

[24]   This short text signed by Hessel, Virilio, and Sloterdijk highlights our current mindsets as the main problem in solving global planetary crises. The text suggests integrating hope into our approach and also addresses the interdependence between global socio-economic issues and environmental issues.

less. That is the entire purpose of Edgar Morin's approach: to prove that it is possible to set a goal, aim at an objective, and follow a set of beliefs that makes sense. We must lead the way for all of these young people who mean well and find themselves involved in myriad initiatives, so that, in becoming united, they may truly come to appreciate their originality of thought and power. Outrage was a first step. It is necessary, but insufficient. We need to follow a thought, a set of beliefs, a will to be different.

Be warned—I am not alleging that *La Voie*[25] is poised to replace *The Bible*. As the author himself puts it, *La Voie* is a contribution, a proposition, and a mere suggestion. It is an invitation to invent the unknown, to uncover human potential. True creation does not know what it will give rise to. Could we have imagined what the *Requiem* would sound like before Mozart wrote and performed it? Could we have imagined that those small societies of hunter-gatherers would come to found cities and civilizations merely some ten thousand years later? The future is not contained within any political agenda, within any to-do list of any hardworking administrator.

Post-historical?

It is a mistake to believe that human history can be summed up in eight thousand years from the beginning of the Neolithic period. We lived through one hundred and fifty thousand prehistoric years. We need this historical dimension to

---

[25]   Morin, Edgar. *La Voie: Pour L'avenir De L'humanité*. Paris: Fayard, 2011. Print.

adequately contextualize our faith in the improbable and the importance of the change to come. Let's put an end to Fukuyama and his clumsy Hegelian fantasy of the end of history,[26] which is poised to emerge through the power of some magical formulas and would come under the delightful guise of what one calls "liberal democracy." We must now conceive of history not so much as a string of time that stretches from one end of time to the other—between an uncertain origin and an eschatological end—but rather as a winding ribbon, coiled into a spiral, which calls to mind the double helix at the root of all life.

We are currently creating a sort of *hereafter* of history. Morin speaks of "meta-history" inscribed within the pulse of human creativity. The world is in movement; it is deep, tectonic, and unpredictable. The improbable occurs. The *new* is emerging and we are going to come out of this global Age of Iron,[27] suggested in the past by Voltaire, and in which we still find ourselves today. The reform of knowledge, the reform of thought, the reform of minds—and therefore the reform of education, without which the other reforms cannot occur and vice-versa—are, as a result, quite urgent. Morin insists on it and I like his line of thought: there is, on

---

[26] This is a reference to Francis Fukuyama's 1989 essay "The End of History" (from *The National Interest* or to the eponymous book from 1992): Fukuyama, Francis. *The End of History and the Last Man.* New York: Free, 1992. Print.

[27] Possibly a reference to Voltaire's 1736 poem, "Le Mondain." Specifically, to this passage: "Ce temps profane est tout fait pour mes moeurs... / O le bon temps que ce siècle de fer." "In the 1730s, [Voltaire] drafted a poem called "*Le Mondain*" that celebrated hedonistic worldly living as a positive force for society, and not as the corrupting element that traditional Christian morality held it to be" (Shank, J.B., "Voltaire", *The Stanford Encyclopedia of Philosophy (Summer 2010 Edition)*, Edward N. Zalta (ed.), URL = <http://plato.stanford.edu/archives/sum2010/entries/voltaire/>.)

the one hand, our desire to revise all established truths, and, on the other, our faith in the improbable.

I personally experienced this faith in the improbable. It was in Marseilles during the summer of 1940—that murderous, terrible, humiliating summer, which was poised to mark the end of all democracies. France: defeated. England: nearly invaded. Russia: turned Nazi (and thereby demonstrating all of the perversity of its true democratic system)… We had failed in our attempt at making democracy triumph, but held fast to the feeling that democracy was, after all, the only victory of that ignoble slaughter that was the Great War. Despair was rather in fashion around that time and that is when I came to Walter Benjamin again.

We had the opportunity to spend a few hours together in Marseille, and I remember very well feeling that I was dealing with someone who was depressed, who no longer had faith, who didn't entertain a desire to find a solution anymore. I, on the other hand, a perky twenty-three-year-old, was telling him that everything would be all right, that things would work themselves out and eventually fall into place. General de Gaulle's call for Resistance, in which I planned on taking part, was ringing in my mind. I professed to Benjamin my certainty in the improbable before any of it came to be—all that we did not know then but that came to be. I wasn't very precise or very clear, but I maintained that sense that we could not lose hope definitively.

This feeling has accompanied me through all of my setbacks: during the war, in which I should have lost my skin, and then, much later, during times that seemed terrible to me like the 1980s (Thatcher and Reagan); times in which free market economic policies were infecting and inundating everything, rotting away everything I had fought for.

If hope is our enemy, where does that leave the revolution?

Jean-Claude Carrière is more skeptical than I am. He believes that we must beware of optimism and invites us to follow Bhagavad-Gita, who says, "Hope is our enemy." For if we hope for something outside of ourselves to occur, we may very well wait for a long time... If there is a hope, he insists, it can only be hope in ourselves, in our daily toil. "Be the change you want to see in the world," as Ghandi said.

Let's also remember Thucydides, who, peremptory, impels us to choose, "Do nothing or be free"—by which he means that being free is a constant fight. If we do nothing, we shall be engulfed by greed, ambition, all the pettiness and mediocrity that surrounds us. We will be swallowed whole, engulfed, and it will result in a world crisis. Therefore we should, on the modest level of our little individual paths, work and fight tirelessly. That's the first condition. And we should start in our own backyards. The worst thing would be for the change we seek today to be imposed upon us tomorrow; all-encompassing, necessary upheaval.

To use, as an example, the Arab revolutions, it is evident that the fall of tyrants and the people's aspiration to liberty—people we had considered culturally and politically doomed to still suffer under the yoke of their predatory raïs[28] for many years—are to be celebrated. But the true challenge is now. How can we take advantage of this moment and this change in history without falling back into the same problems? What will happen? Where are the men of law, the legislators so desperately needed there immediately?

In my tiny bestseller, I attempt to consider despair and hope in the light of one another. But to me, it seems that despair is simply a way in which to make a problem insolvable. And yet, it is within despair that there is the possibility for hope or, let's say, for an engagement; something Sloterdijk calls *exercise* or *asceticism*. As it so happens, asceticism can be a way of renouncing many useless things in favor of a focus on other, more important ones. I am firmly convinced that this type of exercise is a notion that would resonate well with a Buddhist mindset, for we find in these ideas the notion, an increased awareness that the problems dealt us aren't simply to be viewed as needing to be resolved; but that they must be accepted, digested, and slowly integrated in order to become solutions.

But in the same impulse, such problems can torment us, shock, and cause upheaval. And it is impossible not to react. We find evidence of this in one of the fundamental teachings attributed to Buddha, and which is actually the basis of Buddhism itself (you will find it in all Buddhist schools, throughout all of history and across the world): *Expect everything from yourself. Gnothi seauton* or *Know Thyself*, is a

---

[28]   Head of state in Arab countries, specifically in Egypt.

similar precept found inscribed at the Temple of Apollo at Delphi.

According to Jean-Claude Carrière, there can be no other form of hope since no divine being is going to come and resolve our problems. And from the moment we believe in an outside source of help, whether from a transcendent or supernatural power, we are lost.

The most common reaction to unacceptable situations, in our Western mind, is a revolution. A certain kind of youth has, at different moments throughout history, had a tendency to believe that revolution is the alpha and omega of all political action. Since we're on the topic, I'd like to suggest to those people to become interested in Dany Cohn-Bendit's tale of "his" May '68 revolution.[29] I believe there are different ways in which to take action, ways which do not necessarily take place on the streets, but which are achieved through the support of well-intentioned, educated men and women who help put in place more than mere legislation.

First, let's ask ourselves, what is a revolution? What is a reform? What is non-violence and progress through non-violence? Forgive me for looking for answers we already have, and I apologize if this sounds cliché, but I must insist on the fact that the outcome of the revolutions of the twentieth century wasn't good. It is obvious now that those movements, whatever their legitimacy or justifications, resulted more often in excesses, despotism, tyrannies,

---

[29] Hessel may be referring to this volume: Cohn-Bendit, Daniel, and Gabriel Cohn-Bendit. *Obsolete Communism; the Left-Wing Alternative.* New York: McGraw-Hill, 1968. Print.

and dictatorships in the name of ideologies which fancied themselves, undoubtedly, grandiose for all of the world's men. The Russian revolution was a phase, an ideal, and as such, brought a lot to the conscience of men. But its actualization into totalitarian oppression is by no means enviable and gulags must be condemned with the same vehemence as all camps in which torture is practiced. This idea of a revolution has somewhat lost its appeal.

Despair overcome

I cried, "Time for outrage!" and it was heard. But, in the end, the most useful message I have for generations to come is a message of courage and resilience. [Georges] Bernanos said, "What we need is hope. And the highest form of hope is despair overcome." And it is true. Faced with the unacceptable, outrage is not sufficient. Not only because Spinoza is right when he claims that it is an unhealthy emotion since it contains hatred. He advises to not become outraged, to not mock, or cry; but to understand instead. Imagine a xenophobe and his becoming outraged at the number of foreigners in his country. There are a thousand stupid, ridiculous, and unhealthy types of outrage.

It's only when the outcome of outrage is a movement toward action that outrage is justified. Even Spinoza admitted that understanding must be accompanied by emotion, as long as it is under the control of rationality. This goes for outrage too. Outrage in and of itself is not a sign of lucidity. It must be accompanied by the correct knowledge of what merits outrage. Outrage cannot emancipate itself from the intelligence of the world—otherwise, it runs on empty. I remain puzzled by the speed at which my little praise of outrage met its success. And even if we recognize how right it struck in French society—and far beyond too—it must not constitute a culmination. Rather, a beginning.

In a society like our own, the (good) reasons for outrage are many, but it would be dishonest to let you believe that outrage is enough to improve a situation.

Outrage remains, however, a positive first step. It is good to rise up, to become aware, to come out of a certain kind of more-or-less resigned indifference, or despondency, and to say to ourselves that it is possible to resist and to fight against what moves us. But it is only just a step in the larger plan, pulling the alarm, "the beginning of the way." This moment in which we are jolted must not prevent our faith in progress. We should never underestimate our ability to accomplish great, just, and important tasks. Who cares if our initial efforts do not result in much? If engagement in this or that cause has not been crowned with success, if we must go back to the drawing board…?

What we must say to ourselves, then, is that our efforts were only a first step and that future circumstances can evolve and become more favorable. I don't deny it's hard to accept such failings. And therein lies my main regret: that I am somewhat able to express myself, but not able to transform my words into actions. I have been involved, many times, in international mediations, and most of the time, those mediations have failed at first. But then they were undertaken a second, and a third time... I sometimes think that they were inefficient and had no decisive impact. The transition from dialogue to reality is, of course, very difficult—especially for someone who is not a political rat, or even a statesman. I can only hope, therefore, that someone might read this book and realize that it is not enough to put forth messages full of hope and faith. Instead, they might realize that those messages need to be taken up by men and women of courage who will not let the difficulties they will doubtless encounter undo them in their attempt at making those values discussed here prevail and be actualized.

The courage of resilience in the face of chaos

To illustrate our refusal at resigning ourselves, let us look back on recent history, namely on the last decade of the twentieth century, from the fall of the Berlin Wall to the election of George W. Bush. Many causes have progressed. There was the conference of Rio in 1992, the one in Vienna in 1993, then Copenhagen in 1994, and Beijing in 1995. All of the world's states were represented during those summits at which it was observed and proven that progress, at least as it pertained to the environment, to human rights, and to the place and role of women in the world, could be made.

That decade really marked an increase in momentum toward the realization of what global challenges we faced. It's during that period, namely, that we realized to what an extent the problem of the environment was paramount. Some think that the 1990s marked the start of a deterioration of the consciences, which would range from a frenzied individualism to a loss of ideals; but that is not what I experienced.

It is certain that, while a newfound freedom was triumphing in Central and Eastern Europe, a reigning free-market economy (in the tradition of the Chicago School of Economics) was unfortunately taking the world by storm, moving quickly toward deregulation.

In 1993, the last conference of the United Nations on human rights was held in Vienna, a conference during which I had the privilege of presiding over the French delegation. It is there that the countries from the South gallantly affirmed to the countries of the North their "right at development," a right which, up until then, had not been considered by the developed countries, headed by the United States, who seemed to take this demand as a misuse of language, and not a right at all. It was in becoming aware of their own rights that those countries earned due recognition, as well as by upholding the notion that pacts made by the countries in the North stipulate that the right to work, the right to a home, to healthcare, were universal and had to be respected everywhere in the world. It was the American Jimmy Carter, president that year, who conceded that the right to development should be considered an inalienable right.

It was a small concession when considering the dramatic situation of the South, but one that had enormous significance, for it demonstrated the will to recognize interdependence and a shared will to live on this planet as a community. Moreover, at the time, the trend was rather negative generally and leaned towards a lack of consideration for the problems of the South, a lack of consideration for a movement toward a more socially minded and regulated economy. But from Rio to Seattle, some of those resolutions, which were rather progressive in spirit, were adopted (or refused, in some cases); for instance, Agenda 21,[30] which was adopted at the summit of Rio in 1992, or the Kyoto Protocol[31] in 1997. Every single time, our progress seemed slight and the demands those texts made were not always respected in the years that followed. But in the end, those texts, those programs, existed. The same goes for the Universal Declaration; it isn't always applied either. But it exists; and there are people everywhere, citizens, NGOs, who adhere to it and demand it be applied.

After all of this, there was this decade, the one that just ended. What a setback. It began with the confusing election of Bush Junior, and was followed, soon thereafter, by the fall of the Twin Towers in New York City. Those years, 2000 to 2010, are depressing. It has been an accumulation of terrible idiocies and unforgivable mistakes made by many of

---

[30]   "Agenda 21 is a comprehensive plan of action to be taken globally, nationally and locally by organizations of the United Nations System, Governments, and Major Groups in every area in which human impacts on the environment. It was adopted by more than 178 Governments at the United Nations Conference on Environment and Development (UNCED) held in Rio de Janerio, Brazil, 3 to 14 June 1992." ("DSD :: Resources - Publications - Core Publications." *UN News Center.* UN. Web. 15 Mar. 2012. <http://www.un.org/esa/dsd/agenda21/>.)

[31]   "The Kyoto Protocol is an international agreement linked to the United Nations Framework Convention on Climate Change. The major feature of the Kyoto Protocol is that it sets binding targets for 37 industrialized countries and the European community for reducing greenhouse gas (GHG) emissions. These amount to an average of five per cent against 1990 levels over the five-year period 2008-2012." ("Kyoto Protocol." *Http://unfccc.int.* United Nations Framework Convention on Climate Change. Web. 15 Mar. 2012. <http://unfccc.int/kyoto_ protocol/items/2830.php>.)

the most powerful countries on this planet. I won't even mention the absurdity of Europe, which naively believed she was already strong enough to attempt expansion to such a ridiculous extent without running the risk of dissolving in the process. The Americans carried at their helm for eight years a man who was, and that is the least we can say of him, void of any common sense. We saw Afghanistan and Iraq become a playground for neocolonial nonsense. It has been a truly terrible time—a vast Ground Zero for thinking and international politics.

If, in contemplating Paul Klee's *Angelus Novus,* so dear to Walter Benjamin, we were to merely tell ourselves, "Progress is coming, but it's rejecting us, and it's about to get much worse," we would have good reason to be discouraged. So, I believe it is opportune to invoke Friedrich Hölderlin, who, in my eyes, is the greatest German poet, and says: "But where danger is, grows the saving power also." Is this old man, who only has a few years left to live, taking refuge in a comfortable and lazy utopia? No, this message of faith rings true to my ears.

The worst is not always certain. It is likely—in the same way that the improbable must be held as certain.

Interdependence[32]

[…]

From the weariness of forgotten peoples
Vainly would I liberate mine eyelids,
Or would keep my startled soul at distance
From the silent fall of far-off planets.

Many fates with mine are interwoven,
Subtly mingled flow the threads of being,
And my share in it is more than merely
One life's narrow flame or thin-toned lyre.

---

[32]   Hofmannsthal, Hugo Von. *The Lyrical Poems: Hugo Von Hofmannsthal. Transl. from the German with an Introd. by Charles Wharton Stork.* Trans. Charles W. Stork. New Haven [u.a.: Yale Univ., 1918. Print.

Three

The Strength of Compassion

"Nothing is impossible to the will of men as long as their will is strong."[33]

The powers that threaten us today aren't very hard to identify. They draw their power in the *libidos* of the generations that came after us. There is the *libido possidendi*,[34] firstly, which has taken, over the course of the last few decades, a global dimension and has led to a smaller and smaller minority of people benefiting from some fabulous riches—real and virtual—and who now have no other objective than their own advancement.

---

[33] Quote from *Danse avec le siècle* by Stéphane Hessel
[34] The lust to possess, or greed

What also threatens us is the unscrupulous exploitation of nature's resources, which are considered to be unlimited and destined to fill the growing needs of the human race. Our oversight was criminal. We took too long to perceive nature's limits. May our eyes finally be opened to what we can justifiably demand while ensuring the everlasting nature of its prosperity.

And then there is the *libido dominandi*, that thirst for power, which transforms the political leader into a tyrant, the citizen into a subject, and which is characteristic of a certain male mentality.

I'd suggest fighting both those 'lusts' with compassion, which we experience more fully than mere sympathy and which is less offensive than pity for those who are the object of it. I've learned, from Régis Debray, all about the intricacies inherent in brotherhood. How can we all be brothers when we are constantly setting each other apart from one another by our differences? By looking deeply inside ourselves, we can find treasure troves of compassion for those "others" who come to us—I'm thinking, for example, of asylum seekers who come to the wealthy—and whom we have certain advantages over. My friend Bernard Cordier, the most 'human' of all psychiatrists, is convinced that by paying attention to the troubles of others, through a gesture, a kind word, an act of compassion, a gift, we improve our own well-being.

We need not reinvent the wheel however, let us *retell* instead. Those who wish to change the world, and man, are right; it must be done, of course, but not simply by wiping the slate clean of everything we have learned. "To change" is to learn from our past experiences so as to not persist down the wrong path. It begins with the self. The notion of "compassion," and that word "care," a famous concept in Anglo-Saxon sociology, signifies and symbolizes solidarity by definition for me.

In many ways, and for better or for worse, compassion connotes being together in the same passion. Even if, of course, that word still carries some connotation of pity from its original Christian usage. "Sympathy" is too easy; it does not require us to be truly engaged. So "sympathy" is not sufficient and "pity" hurts the "other," since he or she is considered inferior. In compassion, we find both the will to "accompany" and the will to change, and a wish for society to take a more just, more respectful course. Such is the strength of compassion. There is no energy more powerful in changing a human society than the unshakable will of its constituents and their mutual solidarity.

Interdependence and solidarity

Jean-Claude Carrière and I were discussing Buddhist thought. He was explaining its three concepts to me: impermanence, interdependence (which is the basis of ecology and an obvious fact to all Buddhists since the start), and non-violence. What immediately resonated within me was the idea of interdependence.

And indeed, the Collegium International, where I regularly unite with my colleagues Michel Rocard, Edgar Morin,

Henrique Cardoso, René Passet, Mary Robinson, Peter Sloter-dijk, Milan Kučan, Michael Doyle, and so many others from so many different countries, voluntarily chose to tackle this rather new concept in political science.

A few words, in passing, on the Collegium: it looks to fill the need we have for a collective intelligence in approaching our contemporary issues. At the Collegium, we believe that the questions we confront require that individuals with very different but equally important experiences work together. Certain of those individuals have had experiences in abstract philosophical thought, economic theory, and politics; others have had the experience of society directly because they have led their countries. Such have been the ethical, scientific, political reasons for the Collegium International's existence for ten years now—to bring individuals, who have been heads of state or government, and individuals who have led independent yet deep reflections on the great problems facing the future of humanity, in a dialog with each other, a dialog so that they may answer each other, listen to each other. They may come from different walks of life, wear different political colors, but when they come together, it is a concern for the collective future of humanity alone that motivates them. It is a complex and ambitious objective—for many horrible things have been done in the name of good for humanity; but it still is, in all honesty, the only cause that matters.

At the start of the new millennium, our first effort was to draft a "Universal Declaration of Interdependence." It was the very first text upon which we all agreed, thanks to the talent of its writer, Mireille Delmas-Marty. Our second idea was to propose to the General Assembly of the United Nations a vote, from representatives of all people and of all the world's countries, on this completely new idea in the realm of international relations. At the same time, on the eve of September 11, it seemed to us that, in such a difficult climate, the evident connection between interdependence and solidarity needed to be highlighted; in other words, solemnly recognizing the interdependence of the inhabitants of this planet would perhaps finally pave the way for some much needed solidarity.

There are, of course, many ways in which the term "interdependence" can be used; whereas there is, in my opinion, only one way in which to apply "solidarity." And since we were on the topic of Buddhism, interdependence can mean becoming aware of the fact that we all depend on each other. The Dalai Lama often says interdependence requires moderation of the ego's expansion, and that is certainly important; yet coming to the realization that we are all interdependent can also be tinged with regret, for it requires of us to resign ourselves to not being independent. I believe that if we, and the autonomous animals we are proud to be, are to experience interdependence as the opposite of independence, which we could not possibly give up, interdependence takes on a restrictive, nearly negative meaning. On the other hand, accepting and recognizing from the start that each person, each community, each nation is a part of a larger whole, enables us to move past the illusion that is independence. And then interdependence opens a world of possibilities.

Interdependence, as a result, is not opposed to the independence of the elements that construct it. It is instead a flexible whole, within which many independent elements can find a place and move freely, as long as they do not take themselves too seriously. Our dear friends, who are supporters of national sovereignty or of the separation of cultures, of religions, who refuse the very idea of a connection, are utterly fooling themselves. A nuclear reactor that blows up in Ukraine, an Icelandic volcano spitting up scoria and ash into the stratosphere, the Arab Spring,[35] a rise in ocean levels due to global warming, a song that has caught on... no country is an island, not even England; and no actual or imaginary Maginot Line will stop an atomic cloud, the migration flows, the rise of water levels, the propagation of a "Yes We Can." An interdependent planet represents a risk, a danger, maybe; but it is an undeniable reality.

Getting with the times:

the horizons of the impossible

Regard for others is nothing new or innovative. It's an old concept present in all religions, and in a certain number of philosophies—love, friendship, tenderness, seduction, are so many influences whose scope we must fully consider in order to avoid focusing on the frustration that results from our unfulfilled desires.

---

[35]   The expression denotes the series of revolts and protests that have marked the Arab world since 2010.

To outrage and its redemptive powers, we must also add the need for individual growth and, as of now, encourage a different type of education in preparation for life and the world. To "work on oneself," an expression somewhat over-used by magazines and hijacked by pop psychologists, is not a phrase altogether devoid of meaning. Peter Sloterdijk's book, *Tu dois changer ta vie,*[36] resembles a sort of grammar of the various exercises human beings have engaged in for nearly three thousand years in their attempts at morphing into persistent individuals with the ability to rise to the standards of the world they live in.

We are indeed witnessing a strange kind of growth—as the world becomes smaller from the impact of ever faster and more instantaneous technologies, the dimensions of the worlds of each individual have tremendously expanded.

Slotderdijk talks, in his book, about this global shift toward expansion and the new concerns it brings. The first empires, which fully understood the extent of the diversity of people, languages, ideas, and the universe, brought about the first great ideas. China, India, ancient Iran, the prophets of Ancient Palestine and the Greeks, the Egyptians—all of those civilizations left behind their own particular and yet compa-rable tradition, one which places at its center attempts toward improvement—most often in the case of the elite classes, who sought to develop their souls to match the broad shape their world had taken. Our duty is to take up where they left off with

---

[36]   Sloterdijk, Peter. *Tu dois changer ta vie: De L'anthropotechnique.* Paris: Libella-Maren Sell, 2011. Print.

those traditions by building them into our plans for modern pedagogy.

As a matter of fact, Sloterdijk believes exercise should be reintegrated into the education of young people. According to him, the essential flaw of all philosophies developed by enlightened thinkers for the past two hundred years is that this particular aspect of our lives has been neglected—probably because of a rejection of medieval teaching practices and of the absurd scholastic dressing that came along with it. But determination alone cannot lead us to develop in this way. Meditation cannot be learned in one lesson, not any more than painting, writing, or arithmetic. We cannot perform moral acts solely based on our determination to do so, as Kant proposed it. Rather, virtuous actions will more likely be found to arise out of a careful routine we have developed, one in which we have learned to approach trouble with a similar mindset as when encountering the ordinary. It is the alchemy of life. We bring ourselves to believe that the resources needed to shape our bodies and minds happen to be within our reach.

Of course, this requires courage. In fact, at the start of any undertaking, when we approach the horizon of the impossible, it is usually discouragement that wins. But in the same way that outrage transforms resentment into constructive action, "holding superior moral views are already a type of fight against discouragement" (Sloterdijk). Sloterdijk is talking here about the courage to outdo ourselves. This idea of not giving up fostering this will within each of us, within ourselves—not an aspiration toward power, possession, and ambition, but rather toward moral beauty.

How do we ensure society does not step in and stifle this raise in awareness, this impulse toward mobilization against the unacceptable, this faith in ourselves? Solutions already exist, but they are still seeking users. There are already new approaches, new technologies, new modes of production, or consumption. But those solutions must still reach beyond the select circle of its initiated few.

Sloterdijk shared with me his experience at a conference on Werner Sobek, one of the greatest contemporary architects, that took place in his Karlsruhe School. Sloterdijk was full of wonder at the fact that, for a full week, the entire school had fed off that pulse; students had understood that the intelligence of forward thinkers have already developed an entire range of views and techniques that can be applied tomorrow. I get a similar feeling from reading Edgar Morin's book *La Voie*, which does not only speak of those things that are going very badly, but also shows a certain numbers of cases, efforts, which are at the root of actual improvements. It is a way of rekindling faith in the possibility of metamorphosing ourselves.

Faith in the improbable

Edgar Morin's reasoning is fascinating. We have often discussed his intellectual and philosophical development as a sociologist. He explains, as it were, that all of his works look to answer those three essential questions by Kant: "What must I do? What can I know? What can I believe in?" And, like Kant, he encountered the idea that, to be able to answer those questions, we must answer yet more complex questions. We must know what human beings are, what they are capable of, the truth at the heart of all beings. And that is why, ever since *L'Homme et la mort*,[37] *Le Paradigme perdu*,[38] and other books that followed, Edgar Morin has been interested in human nature. A question as eternal as the barrel of the Danaids[39]: to know what we are and what we can be, and to shed light on how multifaceted we all are. His dialectic is as follows: each value carries with it its opposite. We are, consequently, all at once the *homosapiens*, equipped with reason and capable of madness; the *homo fabe* who builds tools and myths; the *homo economomicus* who pursues material interests; and the *homo ludens* who enjoys life, play, and his peers. And then, of course, there is poetry (prose for our obligations, poetry for all that we do out of love, in communion with others), the marvelous poetry we carry within our very selves: the poetry of texts, the poetry of life.

It is this very reflection that inspired Edgar Morin's two books, *Introduction à une politique de l'homme*[40] and *Pour une politique de civilisation*,[41] and also the impetus to move past the the issues of human beings alone. To delve into the heart of our problems, we must, according to Morin, and as

---

[37]   1951 (first edition); Morin, Edgar. *L'Homme et la mort*. Paris: Éditions Du Seuil, 1976. Print.

[38]   1973 (first edition); Morin, Edgar. *Le Paradigme perdu: La Nature humaine*. Paris: Éditions Du Seuil, 1979. Print.

[39]   In Greek mythology, the Danaids were condemned to fill a leaking barrel for all of eternity.

[40]   1969 (first edition); Morin, Edgar. *Introduction à une politique de l'homme*. Paris: Éditions Du Seuil, 1999. Print.

[41]   2002 (first edition); Morin, Edgar. *Pour une politique de civilisation*. Paris: Arléa, 2002. Print.

difficult as this may be, develop a deep understanding of the planetary era in which we find ourselves; one that began with the conquest of the Americas, and which continues today in the shape of globalization. This really struck me because it is a point he holds in common with Sloterdijk, who similarly began to seriously consider the issue of globalization, first in his *Palais de cristal*[42] and then in his *Sphères*[43] trilogy.

Such an undertaking is arduous, for it is not sufficient to simply describe the intensification of fluctuations, the permeability of borders, or the narrowing of the space-time continuum on our planet to explain both the nature of the phenomenon that is globalization and its deep impact on the mind and the functioning of man. We live in an intensely complex and uncertain epoch in which each thing impacts the next. I agree with him, however, that most puzzling is the fact that we no longer cradle this sense that progress will naturally guide us toward what is best—we no longer see the outlines of a desirable horizon toward which we must steer ourselves.

In the end, the point of *La Voie*, and of the magnificent concept at its heart, is the following: in the most likely course of events, disaster is a certainty. A smart observer, given the right information in the right time and place, can guess what the future holds, the most likely course of things. And

---

[42]   Sloterdijk, Peter. *Le Palais de cristal: À l'intérieur du capitalisme planétaire.* Paris: Hachette Littératures, 2008. Print.

[43]   Sloterdijk, Peter. *Bulles: Sphères, microsphérologie.* Paris: Pauvert, 2002. Print. / Sloterdijk, Peter. *Globes: Macrosphérologie : Sphères, tome II.* Paris: Libella-Maren Sell, 2010. Print. / Sloterdijk, Peter. *Écumes sphérologie plurielle.* Paris: Éditions Maren Sell, 2005. Print.

right now the revelation is grim. What is most likely, is the continued degradation of the biosphere, nuclear proliferation and dissemination, and a deepening of the crisis—not only the economic crisis; but all crises touching civilization. Consider the irony of fate: despite the good that came from the fall of Stalinist communism, two paradoxical though mutually beneficial ills have arisen. And yet, the improbable *will* occur—it is a certainty. The example that Edgar Morin often chooses to illustrate this notion of the improbable is Athens: "A beautiful case, in the end, of a pathetic little city that was able, twice, to resist the gigantic empire that was the Persian Empire. And yet even after the second Median war, Athens was taken, pillaged, burned, all seemed lost... But suddenly, the Greek navy ambushes the Persian navy at Salamis and destroys it entirely. Athens resists, and some year later, we are still enjoying their legacies of philosophy and democracy."

There are other, more recent examples of the improbable. In September 1941, the Nazi army was outside of Moscow, after the Soviet government had fled to the other end of the Urals. Suddenly, there occurred an unexpected meteorological event: a precocious and harsh winter that froze the German army at Moscow's doors. Remember too that Hitler had planned his offensive in May 1941, but was forced to delay operation Barbarossa for a month because Mussolini, who had gone without his permission to engulf himself into the conquest of Greece, and who had been held back in the Albanian mountains by a small Greek army, had had to call Hitler to the rescue. They wasted a whole month fighting Serbian and Balkan resistance. What's more, Stalin, at that time, learned through his agents in Japan that the Japanese wouldn't attack Siberia. Suddenly, he found himself free to mess around with the new troops from the Far East, and then suddenly this demented paranoiac became incredibly lucid and named an excellent general (Joukov) to steer his armies; the general counter-attacked and knocked the German army back some two hundred kilometers. Two days later, Japan launched its attack on Pearl Harbor and the United States entered the war. In brief, what became most probable now was that a Nazi victory was improbable.

Metamorphosis and strategy: La Voie *by Edgar Morin.*

In his account, Edgar Morin presents the problem in simple terms: "How are we to change our ways?"[44] Compassion fills a singular role. But if we are indeed this fast train traveling furiously along the rails, how can we change the course of history and switch tracks without being doomed to derail? Humankind has certainly corrected course throughout its history, and at the root of any of its major changes, we often find a person, an individual. The prince Shakyamuni, who became Buddha, is at the origin of an expansive religion that is thousands of years old. Jesus of Nazareth was a little Jewish shaman who only had a few disciples at the time of his death, but of whom one (Saul, also known as Paul) founded this new Universalist

---

[44]   The French word Hessel uses here is *Voie*, which is supposed to allude to the title of Edgar Morin's book (which translate literally to "The Way"). Throughout this passage, Hessel is playing on words, switching back and forth between two definitions of *Voie*: 1. Way(s) and 2. Railway tracks.

religion, which spread across the entire world. And there is the case of Mohammed, which is yet more surprising: chased out of Medina, he sought refuge in an old widow's home, and poof, he too founded a universal and expansive religion.

All said and done, we find that the elements of our lives we consider most established began as aberrations.

Such is the case for capitalism, which arose as a byproduct of feudal society, and was developed, with the help of the royalty, following demands for increased commerce and luxury products. Such is the case for socialism too, which germinated in the minds of a few individuals considered completely zany at the time—Marx, Fourier, Proudhon. And yet, over the course of a few decades only, socialism, for better or for worse, established itself as a formidable force. First conclusion: the issue we face today is not whether or not to be realistic. "Being realistic, what a utopia!" said, in essence, Bernard Groethuysen, who had a very remarkable knowledge of German philosophy—both he and Alexandre Kojève have greatly influenced my development.

According to Morin's line of thinking, we owe ourselves not only to criticize impossible utopias, but also realism; and we must hold fast to the belief that there are possible utopias out there—and what he means by that is that there exist potentially valid realities (global peace, victory over hunger in the world) that simply cannot arise at present due to conditions in the world. No state of things is insurmountable. There's only the process and certain forces to contend with. Recognizing that such tectonic forces are at work also means being able to abandon this idea of revolution.

For indeed, revolutions that look to wipe the slate of the past clean are utterly foolish. Not only can we never truly wipe the slate clean, as is proven again and again at the issue of all revolutions, but we must actually look to preserve the treasures of the past. I am not speaking of cultural treasures alone, but of knowledge, expertise, and intellectual assets. Let's take, for example, organic farming—it was only a matter of reasserting the benefits of the methods used by farmers in the past. The contemporary cannot involve a complete rejection of the past, unless we wish to condemn ourselves to becoming completely rootless. This is where Edgar Morin's idea of a metamorphosis, which he speaks of throughout his books and in other contributions, comes from.

The notion of metamorphosis implies the idea of both maintaining one's identity and becoming another at once. It is a deep transformation in which a certain potential is unleashed. The idea here is therefore that we must achieve a metamorphosis; but how? I'd like to invite you now to focus on what is at the very heart of the strength of compassion: Love. And love always says, in the manner of [Emmanuel] Levinas, "After you, gentlemen."

Love Song[45]

How can I keep my soul in me, so that
it doesn't touch your soul? How can I raise
it high enough, past you, to other things?
I would like to shelter it, among remote
lost objects, in some dark and silent place
that doesn't resonate when your depths resound.
Yet everything that touches us, me and you,
takes us together like a violin's bow,
which draws one voice out of two separate strings.
Upon what instrument are we two spanned?
And what musician holds us in his hand?
Oh sweetest song.

---

[45]   Rilke, Rainer Maria. *Ahead of All Parting: The Selected Poetry and Prose of Rainer Maria Rilke*. Trans. Stephen Mitchell. New York: Modern Library, 1995. Print.

Four

Loving Love, Admiring Admiration

It's not always easy to put the great emotions that define our lives—that define us in our own eyes and in the eyes of others—into words, especially when you are not a writer. How do we learn to love? Is it inscribed in our genes? Does it involve a learning period? For my part, I have been a privileged recipient of love. First, however, I must touch upon the ability to admire, which was, for me, more necessary, more stimulating than love itself in living a happy life. I'd like to encourage all practicing educators to start imparting it on their students. The one who initiated me personally in this domain was Ms. Emmy Toepffer, governess to both my brother and me. She was the one specifically who taught me how to replace rage with the appetite to please. Did she lead me down a perilous path in doing so? After all, I was only three at the time and, accordingly, quite prone to anger. At the age of ninety-three, am I now not quite angry enough anymore? Regardless of the answer, it's too late for me to change. So she was the one who led me to discover the pleasure of admiring something. The first view she imparted upon us was the view that our parents were admirable; that they were, in fact, *exceptionally* worthy of our admiration. That view has never been questioned since. She set the groundwork that opened our minds and which would later welcome those individuals to whom our parents introduced us.

It was a time when art was bursting into new fields, widening its scope. Marcel Duchamp became, for the young child that I was, the embodiment of a breaker of taboos with a hardwearing courteousness. Alexander Calder combined grace and cheerful carelessness. Man Ray's smile gave photography a more amusing feel. André Breton was the strict but fair teacher. Beyond those admirable individuals, beings like Walter Benjamin, Gisele Freund, Charlotte Wolff, Jeanne Moulaert, and her brother-in-law Aldous Huxley came to epitomize for me the very notion of the subtle, the sublime, the true, elevating, as they did, all that they held within to the very highest. Through them, I also came to grasp Eros's two-faced and predominating presence.

You can be very serious at seventeen…

In one of her moments of genius one day, Laure Adler asked me how I had come to discover love. I, naïve, told her about my affairs. First, there was this rather painful memory—an account of what can happen to a young boy who is just slightly younger than his classmates. He might notice that they all have girlfriends with whom they perhaps already… Well, he's not sure what they do. He, on the other hand, is not at it at all yet. But there is that pretty girl B., who lives in Gentilly, and whom he accompanies every morning on the metro so he can walk her from her stop to the École Alsacienne, which she attends. One day he writes her a little note, which he forgets in the classroom. The little note gets passed around, falls into the hands of a friend, and now the boy is a fool. It's the first lesson. He discovers that love can turn us into fools.

A few years later, the most extraordinary thing that could happen at the beginning of a young man's adult life happened to me. My mother, who took very good care of her youngest, pointed out a young girl to me. She was about to be sent to boarding school to receive a proper education. She was slightly younger than me. She was my promised. I was not opposed to it, but it was her mother—a beautiful, cultured woman—who captured my interest instead. At the time, she was seventeen years older than me. What a marvelous adventure it was for a young boy of seventeen to have a thirty-four year old 'friend' at the *Jardin des modes!*[46] By dousing me with love, she taught me sex. I'd pick her up at Condé Nast and she'd initiate me to all of the secrets of the female body a young lad of seventeen, who was still a virgin, could ever dream of knowing. When, once, having crossed France by foot from Paris to Cahors, having left her

---

[46] A French fashion magazine for women

in her train but having returned briefly to fetch a forgotten book and having found her in tears—tears she attributed, prideful, to regrets over our separation—I experienced a height of romantic exaltation that has remained since then unforgotten. That is when I realized that love is an art. With what gentleness and deep respect for that boy—for indeed you are no longer a child at seventeen, but you are certainly not a man either—she went about it all…At seventeen, you are just starting your life, you are shy, you are…stuttering. Above all, however, you do not know at all how to go about it with a woman. You think that love is a word, an emotion, and you tend to forget all of the things that can grow out of it, as, for instance, physical possession. That revelation completely rattled me. I considered at once the incredible breadth of love, all of its diverse facets. At the time, the most surprising were for me the ones that hid in the innermost recesses of romantic feeling.

There are perhaps as many different types of relationships as there are of possible combinations of human beings. For it isn't simply a fragile alchemy between two souls that pine for one another, search for one another, find one another that occurs; it is a more complex sort of relationship, a three-sum of sorts: "There is you, there is love, there is me…"

In those love-induced tears of a mature woman twice my age, maybe surprised all of a sudden by the affection she felt toward her young lover, there was for me an entire mysterious world blooming—from intensity of feeling, ambivalence of emotion, and the insouciances of love, to a certain romantic gravitas.

The following year, at eighteen, I was engaged in the pursuit (a laborious one at that) of a young woman encountered in a crowd of first years,[47] whom the second years, from the height of their extra years, were pursuing joyously and relentlessly. I had hardly caught a glimpse of her, had hardly heard her speak, had hardly been awestruck by her words and their style, that I knew I had to convince her to have me. This meeting was a coming together of all of my senses and emotions. That kind of love knows no bounds, so invested is each party in considering the other as an infinite task to be fulfilled. And we did, I think, accomplish the task well, bringing into the world one girl and two boys over the course of the first sixteen years of a marriage that would last forty-seven, interrupted only by numerous absences for which the war was to blame. I've often spoken of those years of my life: our camping trip to Hera's temple at Olympus, our wedding at Saint-Maixent-L'École, being reunited in Marseilles, then in Lisbon, and eighteen months later in London, our New York years, our Vietnamese year, our five-year assignment in Algiers, and our four years in Geneva.

Sentimental education

I tend to think that what life has of most essential to offer lies in the contact that can occur between two human beings, between two lives that converge and have something to offer each other, two lives that come together to build something.

---

[47]   The word Hessel uses is *hypokâgne*; a term used to refer to first years in their preparatory course for the arts at the École Normale Supérieure.

This happened with V. We had many happy years together. Though, missing from that happiness was perhaps what happened to me a few years later with C. There was a certain level of unexpectedness perhaps, it occurring all at once and just like that, like a revelation of sorts—inexorable, inevitable. With C., it was a love at first sight that I was sadly unable to keep to myself. My wife knew about it because I did what you should never do. I gave her the slip one day, leaving for her a small note that read, "I am now completely taken with someone else, therefore I am leaving," and left her out cold. I still regret the impulse. I bear a heavy guilt for this, naturally, and always have. But I had underestimated my wife's extraordinary strength, for when I returned, three days later, sheepish and admitting my mistake and the desire to take up life in common again, she accepted—on the condition that I might not see the other woman anymore; a condition I neither really wanted nor was able to respect. The whole affair wasn't easy for either of them, or for me, but C. held fast. She had her own life, a job she liked, and a man who gave her a child.

There never was a complete break between us. There were merely long periods of time during which we wouldn't see each other, but when those periods came to an end, we would find each other again. You might see this as a typical cases of adultery, but it was much more complex than that. A love that survives separation, diverging lives, for all of those years, becomes an integral part of your life's story.

I met C. for the first time in 1950, in a hallway of the ministry of Foreign Affairs. She was a young girl, perhaps already a young woman, whose sight caused my body, for the first time, that reaction described by August von Platen in the following line: "The man who has once fed his eyes on beauty / Moves by that very act into death's keeping." No one has better communicated such a moment than Gustave Flaubert, whose statue adorns the Port of Trouville where I am currently writing these pages. Let me share with you this passage of splendid psychological substance in his *Sentimental Education*:

"Never before had he seen such a lustrous dark skin, such a seductive figure, or more delicately shaped fingers than those through which the sunlight gleamed. He gazed with amazement at her workbasket, as if it were something unusual. What was her name, her place of residence, her life, her past? He longed to become familiar with the furnishings of her apartment, with the dresses that she had worn, with the people whom she visited; and the desire of physical possession yielded to a deeper yearning, a painful and boundless curiosity."[48]

Was she exceptionally beautiful? I am not certain. What I am certain of is that a signal traveled from her to me—a signal, which has never failed us since. We even had this romantic temptation once to end it all together. I left my wife to join her, but she fell ill precisely when she and I were supposed to leave for Samos together. Caught in that early stage of love where everything is brutal and intense, we had decided we should die young. We knew it was folly,

---

[48]   Flaubert, Gustave. *Sentimental Education: The Story of a Young Man*. Whitefish: Kessinger, 2008. Print.

of course, and a misdeed, at least morally, so it had to happen fast. Love and death—this impulse toward death, toward the absolute, had occasioned in the bewilderment induced by our completely uncontrollable love, and was pushing us toward that Greek Island to end our days there. We believed we had been made to die.

Today she is eighty-three years old and I am ninety-three, and life gave us the gift of reuniting us after we were both widowed. No sooner had my wife been taken from me due to illness, did this connection, which has never faded since, give rise to a second marriage, to a high degree of conjugal joy in which I recognize the markings of this blessed life, of this happiness I must owe to some guardian angel no doubt, this happiness no one could possibly deserve. What an immense joy it was to be reunited again and again throughout the years. Nowadays things are simpler. If I travel to Sarajevo, she comes with me, and when I return from a trip, the first thing we do is tell each other, "Now, to the sheets, to the bed, to being alone!" A balance has been created, a marvelous balance.

In addition to those edifices of love, I shall briefly touch upon another, more secret, more fleeting, more powerful one—I am speaking of Eros. I am speaking of sex. During a visit to Algiers, a friend of V.'s told me, as she was departing, "I need you as my lover." Nothing could have prepared me for this phrase. Her need for our meeting was strong enough to ensure it occurred and to make me discover, for the first time, how a beautiful woman can reach incredible heights of rapture, how then all modesty vanishes, leaving room only for elation. But the dangers such a love can entail also make you shudder.

That is the kind of creature we are. That is, too, what love's great expectations have taught me. Eros, who is both the direct son of Chaos (first in Gaia and Ouranos' divine genealogy), but also the secret son of Ares and Aphrodite, has put me through some hard times. His effect on each of us is the best example of the complexity of our natures, which are constituted not only of knowledge and reason, but also of our physicality and heart, our imagination and anxieties. What do we mean by love anyhow? To *make love* does not necessarily mean we are *in love*. What is the role of sex in our lives, so rich in intense pleasures and cruel traps? The man's ambition in learning to make his partner climax is one exercise of which Peter Sloterdijk specifically points out the importance; to love is certainly more important than being loved. But then again, passion can become destructive; we never love enough, or well enough. The different periods of my life all bear the indelible mark of how I have loved, rather than how I was loved.

Eros and Thanatos

In my teenage years, in London, I discovered that Greek mythology provides us with the most precious information we can find on love's manifold facets, how it relates to life experience and to our poetic imagination. I had been welcomed there by a cousin of my mother's in a suburb with an alliterative name, West Wickham. There were two

boys a little younger than me, John and Basil, who initiated me to cricket, propelling me deep into British culture.
I was enrolled as a student at the London School of Economics, whose buildings weren't too far from Guildhall
Library.

More often than in LSE's classrooms, I would set myself
up in that public library and I would devour there the writings of Diodorus Siculus and Apollodorus of Athens. I'd follow the genealogy of the gods and heroes and the tales of
their battles and passions. I began with the most recent, the
heroes of *The Iliad* and *The Odyssey*, and worked my way back
to the most ancient, to the genitors of that impressive line-
age. The gods of Olympus were very close to Homer's heroes;
their parents, the Titans and Titanesses, were couples who,
though reduced to silence, were cloaked in great and pres-
tigious symbolic status; among them, Chronos, the master of time—not the time it actually is, but time that passes
inexorably; among them Japet, whose son Prometheus went
to face his cousin Zeus and, thanks to the fire he robbed from
the immortals, gave humans the power to grow in strength
and wisdom; and among them still—since each Titan had
a Titaness for a sister—Mnemosyne, powerful symbol of
memory. She is the one from whom the Muses descend. Yes,
memory is the source of all artistic imagination, of poetry for
a start: Calliope, the eldest, mother to Linos and Orpheus.

We must look back farther still, to the parents of the
Titans, to the Earth and Sky, Gaia and Ouranos, who made
order emerge from Chaos, and who accomplished that
necessary task with the help of two fraternal figures, Eros

and Thanatos, or love and death. Those two are at work at any given moment in our history, both of them freeing us from isolation. One draws us out of our young timidity and thrusts us into the pursuit of another; the other expects us patiently, certain to welcome us one day.

But Helen, in all of this, (for me, Helen was my mother) what was her role? We must hark back to her mother Leda, who like many, was coveted by Zeus. In order to possess her, the king of the Gods took the form of a swan. Two of my favorite poets, the Irishman Yeats and the German Rilke, have dedicated a poem to this event. The first poet alludes to the offspring issued from that union; offspring that will engender the death of the kindest of kings, Agamemnon. The second merely limits himself to evoking the pleasure derived by the god; a pleasure we readers share too, entirely. Eros is utterly present and we know full well that Thanatos will come to claim his victims sooner or later. Indeed, four children will be begotten from this passionate embrace: the Diascuri, who were placed in the cosmos— two boys, one of whom is immortal (Castor) and the other forced to share mortality with him as well (Pollux), and two girls, Clymenestre and Helen.

To see Helen is to become irrevocably engaged; just as the Greek heroes of *The Iliad* were, when the Trojan Paris deprived her husband of her and they engaged themselves to return her to him, thereby initiating a war that would last over a decade. Who is to blame for all of this? The answer is Aphrodite, of course. It is she—chosen like Paris, as the most beautiful, the one to whom the apple tossed by Eris during Thetis and Peleus's nuptials was awarded—who promised him the favors of the most beautiful of all women, who could be no other than Helen.

I am recounting all of this to shed some light on the relationship between love and death as it is found in Greek mythology, or in the Ireland that Robert Gravers initiated me to—the Ireland of Assur and of his legend of Gilgamesh—to shed some light on the relationship between an impassioned life and quasi-unachievable immortality. A true hero—as they were found in the tales of King Arthur—would be someone who would, after combat, know only love and then death.

On jealousy

But our existence is more complex still. What infiltrates and disturbs this pretty order is jealousy. The "I" retreats into itself, desires others all for itself, rather than for whom they are. Every time I have encountered jealousy in my own love life, whether in myself or in my partner, I have done everything I could to defeat it. I understood its intensity and horror early on, in the tale that puts an end to the twelve labors of Hercules: Hercules falls for Iole, but wants to protect his wife from the centaur Nessus. The latter is vanquished, but hands Dejanira a tunic, which he claims can make love reborn in the heart of the man who wears it. An infamous trap! Nessus was seeking revenge. It was obvious, and only jealousy could have allowed Dejanira to be fooled in such a way. *Oh! Were Hercules to abandon Iole and return to me,* she must have been thinking. This is not the first occasion upon which Hercules switches partners. He is a fertile lover and a countless number of Herculeses can be found across the myths. But Dejanira cannot stand it. And so Hercules follows her request and puts on the fateful tunic. And he that no lion, no hydra, no giant was able to slay, is now so deeply consumed with jealousy that he has no remaining option left but to join Hera who—herself jealous of Amphitryon's wife, whom Zeus had made Hercules's mother during the longest nights of lovemaking that have ever been written about—slaps Alcmene's miraculous little brat with twelve labors, to which a different kind of jealousy will put an end.

So can we learn to love without being jealous? Yes, and I would like to lead by example. Who could I have been—or should I have been—jealous of? Of my older brother, coddled for a rather glorious handicap, epilepsy? It gave him great distinction. You could call it a *grand* ailment. And I was quite small in comparison. Well, no. I experienced him instead as a more fragile brother, whom I could protect in the same way he protected me.

Should I have been jealous of Henri-Pierre Roché, from whom my mother would have desperately wanted a child, and who wouldn't have hesitated, had it succeeded, to leave both my brother and me behind to live that other love more fully? Well, no. I sided instead with her great love, knowing deep within me that she would love me even more and that I would keep her, and that her lover would remain dear to me even if all of her plans were to fail. Of my classmate Robert Decamis, a first year, in love as I was with the arousing V., of whom he managed to be the first love? Again, no. My friendship for him was strengthened. It seemed to me instead that he pathed a way, opened a gate that I was then allowed to enter. Of my wife V., when I, having left Lisbon where I had joined her in March 1941 and having reached New York where her parents were waiting for her, left her behind for London? I learned that she had met someone important in New York, at the heart of that famed group of artists who had been saved by my friend Varian Fry: André Breton, Marcel Duchamp, Claude Lévi-Strauss. Among them was Patrick Waldberg, whose advances she would not resist. I knew nothing about it of course until the day when, V. having joined me in London in November 1942, he caught up with her eight days later. Their relationship did not resume and he and I became the most constructive of friends, so similar were our tastes.

The opposite was, sadly, not the case. I still carry the weight of my infidelities. There were not many, but each left its mark, which troubles my dreams to this day. I could never admit them and had to lie to allay suspicion. Sometimes suspicion was not allayed.

In that respect my second marriage marked an entry into an age of freedom for me. We were both older than sixty. We'd known each other for more than thirty-five years. We had decided, this time, to go to the end together, to remain together until death. But Eros is always present and so I met Christiane. Thanatos will have to wait a little longer.

Are there other outlooks on love?

My mother, so exclusive in her love for her two children and at the same time prepared, as I said earlier, to sacrifice them for a yet more exclusive passion, believed that her Stéphane needed to have a homoerotic adventure early on. She was an avid reader of André Gide and had recommended to me, at 12, to read *Corydon*. In Henri-Pierre Roché's personal library, where I would spend entire afternoons dazzled, there was Cocteau, Artaud, Klossowski, and Leiris.

I only met the opportunity once when, aged twenty-two, I fell into the arms of a young American. It was in Marseilles. France had lost the war. Vichy was collaborating with Hitler; the anti-fascist artists had expatriated themselves to the South of France and feared for their lives and freedom. My father and my brother had been sent to the Camp de Milles, near Aix-en-Provence, for a few months.

I was informed at once of the arrival of this young American at the Hôtel Splendid, a young man tasked with helping those whose artistic and intellectual renown interested the United States (which had not joined the war yet) to leave France for America.

Roosevelt kept an ambassador to Petain in Vichy, the Admiral Leahy. But Roosevelt's wife Eleanor, at the head of the International Rescue Committee, had chosen Varian Fry to accomplish a different mission. And he did an admirable job, helped too little by the American consulate in Marseilles which would have wanted to restrict his mission merely to luminaries such as Breton and his wife Jacqueline, Max Ernst, Victor Serge, Jacques Lipchitz. Fry quickly understood that those most threatened were the Jews, especially foreign Jews, and he successfully helped to send away more than a thousand of them, thereby becoming the only American "Righteous among the nations."

We met in August and thanks to his help, my wife, my in-laws, and myself, were able to leave Marseilles in February 1941—they through Spain, I through Algeria. My relationship with Fry was one of true camaraderie. Whenever he could spare some time from his fundamental task—a task being handled by a brave team among which I had many friends—he would take me with him to visit this Provence he knew very little about and which fascinated him. Over the course of our nights in hotels, I quickly understood that his inclination toward me had a sexual dimension to it, something I had aroused from the depth of the great affection he inspired in me due to the fact that he was not insensitive to our plight.

Those moments are locked away in my memory and today I am unable to tell you how far we went in our embraces. I only know that I never truly developed a taste for them, even if I rank Achilles and Patroclus's encounters highly among the events in this dear Greek mythology.

Mirabeau Bridge[49]

Under Mirabeau Bridge the river slips away

And lovers
Must I be reminded
Joy came always after pain

The night is a clock chiming
The days go by not I

We're face to face and hand in hand
While under the bridges
Of embrace expire
Eternal tired tidal eyes

The night is a clock chiming
The days go by not I

Love elapses like the river
Love goes by
Poor life is indolent
And expectation always violent

The night is a clock chiming
The days go by not I

[49]   Apollinaire, Guillaume. *Alcools: Poems*. Trans. Donald Revell. Hanover: Published by UP of New England [for] Wesleyan UP, 1995. Print.

The days and equally the weeks elapse
The past remains the past
Love remains lost
Under Mirabeau Bridge the river slips away

The night is a clock chiming
The days go by not I

Five

The Joy of Encounters

From whom did I learn to so love loving? Certainly from my mother, who was a woman passionately in love, prepared to sacrifice her children for her passion, but who was also an educator with many talents—the talent, above all, of snubbing Bourgeois morals, of chasing away conformism, of freeing the most poetic of all imaginations, while basing each one of her actions in her innate faith in the ethical commandments of Immanuel Kant's categorical imperative. She taught me, most importantly, how to be happy (if only to become worthy of she who knew how to impart happiness). She taught me to be happy so that I might acquire a sufficient degree of self-confidence so that I myself might propagate happiness and surmount all obstacles encountered between my goals and the efforts required to achieve them.

If I am suggesting to the generations who come after me, and toward whom this message is tentatively addressed, to fully learn the art of admiration and love, it is because I see in both those things the most precious human experience.

To overcome the perils we must expect to encounter (revealed by Régis Debray in his accounts on brotherhood[50]), we shall have to dig into the most ancient resources of our *humanitas*. Let us not be fooled however; there are dangers involved not only in ending the incredible oversight of the wealthy, who have made the economy unmanageable, have disproportionately enriched some and reduced billions of others to destitution, but also in ending the oversight which has caused societies, as they 'progressed,' to become the shameless and forceful exploiters of resources of this unique planet we must claim as our habitat, resources, which have been recognized, too late, as being limited.

And it is to those dangers, identified, described, understood, and denounced at last by the thinkers and poets whom we admire, that the current generation must respond today with a sincere and deep engagement.

The taste for admiration… How did I acquire it? It is, once again, a gift from my mother. A taste I took to naturally, a taste instilled without effort. My mother was, herself, more inclined to admire than to criticize. She was a fervent lover, who sometimes proffered onto her partners a level of admiration beyond what they actually warranted, but, all said and done, it is this ability to find certain individual acquaintances

---

[50]   Debray, Régis. *Le Moment Fraternité*. Paris: Gallimard, 2009. Print.

worthy of admiration that helps us in our attempt at separating the mediocre from the sublime. In the end, we all have a part of mediocrity within us. It's never much fun when it's noticed upon first look. It's more stimulating for all if that part is noticed only after what is admirable in us has been enjoyed.

A taste for others

Admiration: I too am a recipient of it. I've discovered a new way of being heard and welcomed. I have always been warmly received by the public, especially in those schools where I'd been made to come and bear testimony to the Resistance or deportation. But I am now confronted with a different kind of consideration and admiration, which reflects, I think, how my simple words were able to tap into the very core of people's experiences and current dismay.

In the street, strangers will come up to me and say, "You're Stéphane Hessel, aren't you?" Surely, this can be attributed to the impact of television. But above all, I think they approach me because of this feeling of kindred spirits—and for me, this means I have the opportunity today to give back what I once received. All I have to offer is some wisdom my life lent me and the influence the public grants me.

This wisdom is mostly derived from all of the wonderful encounters I have had over the course of my existence. Bookish encounters, for one: the poets Apollinaire, Rilke, Hölderlin, Shakespeare, and Baudelaire, and the philosophers Hegel, Plato, Merleau-Ponty, Nietzsche, and Parmenides.

Reading opens as many new worlds to us as it does appropriate words to describe reality. And then there were encounters with individuals; whether they took the shape of a simple conversation or extended to the warmth of a shared friendship, I have had the benefit of precious intellectual and moral exchanges that have enriched me immensely. I was lucky to follow a path, which, in France, ensures intensity and consequence—*hypokâgne, kâgne,*[51] the École Normale Supérieure with teachers such as Maurice Merleau-Ponty and Léon Brunschvig.

There is within me both a natural interest for philosophy; but also a regret to have had to completely put my learning on hold, to be incapable today of reading modern philosophy intelligently because, very simply put, the concepts are no longer the ones I am used to. I often feel abandoned by contemporary philosophers, and closer to people who are *philosophically inspired*, but who are not literally 'philosophers' in the same fashion as Derrida, for instance.

A mind such as that of Edgar Morin, for instance, who is not strictly speaking a philosopher, but more of a thinker, a totalizing sociologist, is more accessible to me. That being said, when I meet, even for a brief moment, someone like Peter Sloterdijk, a philosopher by profession, I discover a lucid outlook on today's world and on what we can accomplish tomorrow.

I am using Morin as an example again. I always draw great enjoyment from chatting with him, not only because

---

[51]   Those terms correspond to "freshman" and "sophomore," but for students of the renowned école Normale Supérieure in Paris.

he is a friend and a brilliant mind, but above all because he has guided me in my reflections for quite a long time now. It all started in 1958, shortly before I founded the Club Jean Moulin[52] with my accomplice Daniel Cordier. At the time, Morin had taught me to understand this new paradigm: human nature. He had also helped me to become aware of how deeply the values upon which I was trying to build my life, ranging from the Resistance to the fight for human rights through the Universal Declaration, were interconnected. He showed me, most importantly, that this connection needed to be nurtured from time to time, in the light of the evolution of society itself. Today, the world has changed course. Our beliefs have faded, along with the old world. The war had a certain simplicity for us, where the decisions that needed to be made were obvious: to not lose and then, having lost, to still try and win… The simplicity of then is no longer relevant today. It actually seems to me that today, and for the past ten years now, we are somewhat unclear on where our societies are headed.

And Edgar's conclusion on that topic is fascinating. The complexity within which we are operating prevents any dualist views—this side against the other, this social class against the other… Today, what is essential, rather, is to unite all women and men of good will who share one same conscience. We must call to the world to open its heart.

---

[52] Jean Moulin was a French Resistant. The Club, a politically engaged center for thinking, was founded in 1958 (http://chsp.sciences-po.fr/en/fond-archive/club-jean-moulin).

Missionary meditations

I also developed a taste for others in my role as mediator. Somewhere in *Danse avec le siècle* I remember writing this phrase: "There is no such thing as successful mediation. Through its very failure, it paves the way forward toward another, more complex method that will fail in turn. It is through this never-ending sequence that the brave history of our species is written."

My assignments and attempts were very diverse: from the *sans-papiers*[53] in Burundi, and then Burkina Fasso, to the Haut Conseil à l'Intégration[54]… Such diversity allowed me a range of encounters in which I found each to be more enriching than the next.

I remember well, the whole affair of the *sans-papiers* took place in 1996. Ariane Mnouchkine was the one who involved me. She had had the kindness and generosity to welcome three hundred Malian, for the most part, but also some Senegalese and a few Algerians, at the Théâtre du Soleil. Theirs was not a cry of misery; it was, instead, an attempt at reclaiming their dignity. The message was simple: We are being refused papers to which we are entitled. We want documentation, not benefits, and we want it because it is our right.

After taken them in, Ariane Mnouchkine realized that, up against a government like Mr. Alain Juppé's, Prime Minister, and Mr. Jean-Louis Debré's, Minister of the

---

[53]   Undocumented immigrants

[54]   A council that looks into the integration of foreigners. More info here: http://www.hci.gouv.fr/.

Interior, it would be necessary to bring together individuals who had enough pull with leaders to suggest a solution. That is how she came to form that committee. I was the eldest member, and on top of it, Ambassador of France, which tended to have quite an effect. Shortly thereafter I was asked to become the president of that group we would call the *Collège des médiateurs.*[55]

And we presented a simple proposal to the government: of those people, there were about 80% who could be legalized and perhaps 20% who needed to be sent back to their countries. We devised a list of 10 criteria, which would determine whom it was possible and justified to legalize. We, of course, pointed out that not all criteria needed to be met; fulfilling one provided sufficient cause to be legalized. That group of people was one of the most remarkable I have ever been invited to preside over. There was Laurent Schwartz, Edgar Morin, Jean-Pierre Vernant, Lucie and Raymond Aubrac, Pierre Vidal-Naquet, Germaine Tillion, and Paul Bouchet, a remarkable man and statesman, who helped us greatly. There was also Paul Ricoeur, who has died since, as so many other members of that *Collège*. It was a wonderful group with such intellectual and, even, political distinction that we could not conceive that the government would refuse to hear us. Presented with our propositions, however, the government left it to the *préfet*,[56] asking him to "take into our

---

[55] In 1996, a group of 26 men and women in high ranking positions across all of society banded together in defense of immigrants against the then right-wing government. More info here: http://www.bok.net/pajol/college.html.

[56] In France, a *préfet* is a high-ranking civil servant who represents the State at the level of the "département" or the "région" (*The Collins Robert French Dictionary*)

account" some of the things we had suggested. And instead of doing just that, he kept himself entertained by legalizing twelve of the three hundred undocumented immigrants and denying the others. We were furious and spoke out against his action quite a bit. It was a period of fertile encounters with the press.

I had already, some years earlier, taken part in attempts at mediation in Africa, between the Tutsis and the Hutus in Burundi for instance. I have a keen interest in issues of immigration, integration, and in the dignity of those men and women who have made the gut-wrenching decision to leave their home countries and place their fate in the hands of a more hospitable land. And I have always objected to the scandalous manner in which France treats the issue of the right to asylum.

Remarkable friends

My entire life has been inspired by "encounters," whether intellectual or political, literary or sexual, philosophical, or spiritual. In the heat of a conflict or within the tranquility of a friendly conversation, encounters with remarkable friends have fed and continue to feed my reflections. In these past years, some of them have even helped me to refine, confirm, develop, and enrich my view of the world. I would like to acknowledge here those who helped me build this account.

I have known Régis Debray for a very long time—since our adventure at the Club Jean Moulin—and I have a great deal of affection for him. We must remember that my *vivarium* is, after all, the members of the Club Jean Moulin, who remain for me true democrats influenced by Pierre Mendès France. I maintain that he has a too high—much too high—opinion of me. A few years back, he brought together a few of the great Resistants still alive within the context of his journal *Médialogie*. He gave us voice, Daniel Cordier, Yves Guéna, Jean-Louis Crémieux-Brilhac, and me. It was very interesting and fun. Régis Debray is a human being to whom I am deeply attached. As a matter of fact, he did something that I find incredible— he dedicated one of his books to me: *Le Moment Fraternité*. It had never before happened to me. We have done many things together over the course of the years, but the one that marked me the most was our trip to Gaza.

Nineteen-sixty-eight was all about Dany Cohn-Bendit. Of course, I didn't know him beforehand, and I did not actually meet him then either, since I was in Algeria. Our meeting took place some twenty years later when, as deputy mayor, he was put in charge of immigration and cohabitation[57] in Frankfurt. He reached out to me because he knew that I had written a report addressed to Michel Rocard on how to handle the whole issue. We knew each other very indirectly, but we had a strong connection.

We met over those topics—for fascinating political conversations on how to approach issues of immigration, of integration, of life for different cultural communities in the same town. Later, I came to know him as 'Dany le Vert,'[58]

---

[57] He took charge of multicultural affairs in 1989.

[58] Translates literally to "Dany the Green"; Daniel Cohn-Bendit is the most recognizable French figure involved in ecological efforts at this time

the tireless activist who appears every ten years to shake the French and European political scene. As a matter of fact, I took advantage of his last visit to 'greenify' myself by participating, together with José Bové, whom I also know well, in that formidable adventure Dany had set up through Europe Écologie,[59] an impertinent and enthusiastic movement, capable of testing the limits and changing the face of an ossified left, in which I had nonetheless never lost hope.

Dany is, in my mind, of extraordinary political relevance. His breakdown of situations in which we find ourselves always seems the most enlightened to me. As he is, in addition, very frank and direct, and won't take orders from anyone, I find in him a very particular kind of political intelligence. It is no coincidence that he is an ecologist—for the major issue nowadays is the future of our planet. The fact that he does not dissociate the fight against man's destruction of nature from the fight against poverty makes him, in my eyes, a very valuable man in politics. I don't think he really has the makings to be a head of party. As a matter of fact, when he tries to be, it doesn't go very well. He doesn't have the soul of a minister either—of Education or of the Environment, or of anything else. He leaves it to those who have both taste for and competency in such things. He is, however, an incorruptible watchdog, who sounds the alarm on all that is failing, and is a guide steering us toward what must be done.

---

[59]   Organization that brought together the green party and other ecologists and regionalists for the European elections of 2009.

If I have such deep affection for Michel Rocard, it is because he is the man who best embodies the ideas of the left as they were defined by Pierre Mendès France. He is, in my opinion, the true heir of Mendès—with a similar connection to socialism and who holds, at the same time, the view that we need to make socialism work together with a regulated economy. And since we're at it, both Rocard and Mendès France had a similar problem in their respective political lives: Mittérand.

I also met Michel around the time of the Club Jean Moulin, back in the days of the PSU.[60] I'd known his father during the war, quite a remarkable man—a great scientist, very demanding, who had wanted for his son to follow in his footsteps and become a scientist too, instead of a prime minister. It reminds me a bit of that amusing anecdote… In heaven, following the Assumption, the Virgin Mary answers the following to an angel, who is in rapture at seeing the fate of Jesus turned savior of all humanity: "I would have preferred he be a doctor."

I only met that great German philosopher Peter Sloterdijk recently. We met in the context of the Collegium International, in 2008, in Monaco, during a roundtable led by Prince Albert, which was modestly dedicated to the future of the planet. I had read, at the time, Sloterdijk's first book, *Critique of Cynical Reason,*[61] which I had found extremely interesting, specifically because it wasn't conformist in the

60   United Socialist Party

61   Sloterdijk, Peter. *Critique of Cynical Reason*. Minneapolis: University of Minnesota, 1987. Print.

least or, for that matter, rooted in any philosophical tradition of the time. Since 2008, we've had the opportunity to meet again, especially in Karlsruhe where he has invited me. We have a good rapport.

I am no expert in his school of thought, far from it, but our conversations are always very stimulating intellectually and I draw a great deal from them. To me, he is a philosopher in both the literal and the figurative sense. I am particularly intrigued by his way of describing the responsibility of man in performing exercise.

The translation into French, by Olivier Mannoni, of his latest book, *Tu dois changer ta vie,*[62] brought me to an understanding of the methods he creates in seeking to develop a deeper understanding of the types of societies we must build.

It is first of all sadness that the name Jean-Paul Dollé evokes within me, for he passed in the first months of my beginning this book. We did not know each other personally. I had met him thanks to Sacha Goldman in the context of the Collegium, once again. But I immediately sensed that for him philosophy and sociology and even politics were part and parcel. He was someone who believed thought must not remain abstract, but must become actualized, concrete. And in that respect, the few conversations we had were especially enjoyable and very useful.

I first met Laure Adler eons ago and our relationship grew from our shared love for poetry. I think one of my first

---

[62]   Sloterdijk, Peter. *Tu Dois Changer Ta Vie: De L'anthropotechnique.* Paris: Libella-Maren Sell, 2011. Print.

memories of her—and this brings me back to poetry—is of a meeting at the Cabaret Sauvage. She was there, and since she was a redhead back then—she is not any longer—I recited "La Jolie Rousse," staring at her. We began a poetry-based relationship and she became a friend. Later, when she became, for a year, the president at the Seuil Editions, she took the opportunity to publish my book *O ma mémoire*: *La poésie, ma nécessité.*[63] For that, she has earned my deepest gratitude. I must say that, at the time, I had already sent the manuscript to some publishers, but all of the answers seemed alike, that charming letter you love to receive when you are a writer which says: *Your manuscript interested me a lot and touched me deeply too. Unfortunately, no publisher can publish a trilingual book and I am therefore unable to accept it. Thanks for sending.* A few months later, Laure Adler bet on this trilingual book and, in the end, I believe she had nothing to complain about because it sold quite well at the Seuil. The book will reappear in Poche edition soon and has now been translated into German.

I knew of Jean-Claude Carrière only that he had made possible the production of *The Mahabharata*, that he had led interviews with the Dalai Lama, and that he had published many works of fiction (for theater and film) and essays. I remember a saying of his I had heard at some point: *The future is a tradition. How long will it continue to be?* That phrase puzzled me.

---

[63]   Hessel, Stéphane. *O ma mémoire: La poésie, ma nécessité.* Paris: Seuil, 2006. Print.

My exchanges with him enlightened me on the spiritual aspect of this questioning on politics I've committed myself to, in between various revolts, hopes, ecological ambitions, acts of solidarity, and the time spent reviving the notions of interdependence and compassion. His ideas opened up new horizons to me.

I would also like to touch upon two encounters that have left a deep impression on me. Two men without whose intervention I probably wouldn't have become who I am today.

Eugen Kogon—without him, I wouldn't be here. His role, in a decisive moment of my existence, revealed his rare courage even in the heart of one of the most dangerous camps, Buchenwald. Thirty-six of us had arrived there, having left Paris on August 9—fifteen days before the arrival of the Allies—thinking the war was lost for the Nazis. My closest companion was Forrest Yeo-Thomas, who was close to Winston Churchill—a 'bravest of the brave'—and who had been parachuted into France to help Pierre Brossolette flee. Having failed and gotten himself arrested, he was waiting, like me, in Block 17, where the thirty-six of us were being kept. We did not know it, but we had been sentenced to death. When sixteen of us were hung from a butcher's hook, the rest knew there was no other hope than to set up an escape plan. It was Yeo-Thomas's relationship with Kogon that made it succeed—for only three of us. The rest were shot.

Kogon, a Christian resistant of Nazism, had been in the camp since 1939 and had earned a privileged post as the assistant to Dr. Ding-Schuler, the expert typhus resident in our block, a damned place where some SS were conducting lethal experiments on the deported. Kogon presented this perilous proposition to Ding-Schuler: to welcome some allied officers into the block, where young dying Frenchmen lay under the hold of typhus, and send the Frenchmen's bodies to the crematorium under the name of the allied officers who, themselves, would leave for other camps under their new identities. In exchange, Ding-Schuler, who knew that the war was lost, would have those officers take along with them some signed certificates which would attest to the fact that he had done them a favor. The SS only wanted to take two; Kogon made him accept three. The third was myself. In retelling this story here for the thirtieth time, my hand still shakes. Each of those who went to die could have been saved in my place. Without Kogon, and also without Yeo-Thomas, who chose a Frenchman in addition to two Englishmen, my life would have ended.

Eugen Kogon, who I saw far too little after the war ended (three times only in 1945, before my departure for New York), is unforgettable. Coincidentally (my guardian angel dishes such coincidences out by the fistful), it is his son, Michael Kogon, who translated my books *O ma mémoire*: *La poésie, ma nécessité, Time for Outrage,* and *Become Engaged* into German. It is Michael too who made me, in 2001, the recipient of the Eugen-Kogon Prize, from the eponymous foundation. The importance of Kogon in writing the history of Germany is invaluable. Aside from his cultural and political review, *Les Cahiers de Francfort*, which was, for a

long time, very influential in the German-speaking commu-
nity, he most importantly contributed scholarship on the
National-Socialist phenomenon with his remarkable book,
L'Etat SS,[64] which actually features some of our correspond-
ence. It is the work that possibly best describes how the
German youth happened to be so misled by Hitler.

And then there's Walter Benjamin, whose importance
I already touched upon in regards to my intellectual development. I met him when I was seven. I could say so many
things about this exceptional, refined, delicate man—a
philosopher, an art historian, a literary critic, an art critic,
and translator... An altogether a superior spirit. But I often
like to relate the only funny thing that can be related on
him (because there are many dark things too).

We were at home as a family and were involved in a
session of what is referred to as *Bibelstrechen* in which the
participants pick a book (*The Bible* most of the time, but
any other book will do) and then one person slides a knife
between two pages and selects one of them. Then, someone else announces which passage must be read and in
honor of whom (whether that person happens to be present or not). They will say, for instance, "Let's all think of
X and read the 5th line from the bottom" or "Let's read the
4th line from the top of the page on the right" or the left "in
honor of him or her." The reader must read the entire line

---

[64]   English translation: Kogon, Eugen. *The Theory and Practice of Hell: The German
Concentration Camps and the System behind Them*. New York: Farrar, Straus and
Giroux, 2006. Print.

and nothing but that line, even if there is a break and it is the middle of a passage.

That day, we had drawn for Benjamin: "can also be, but with more difficulty, a fool—" and the line ended there.

It reminded me of the first sentence of *Monsieur Teste*, the book by Paul Valéry, which states, "Stupidity is not my strong suit."

Recognize the truth as truth; feel everything in every way, and be nothing in the end--only the understanding of all—when a man rises to this pinnacle, is free, as in all heights, alone, as in all summits, he is united to heaven.[65]

---

[65] http://www.sophia.bem-vindo.net/tiki-index.php?page=Pessoa+Caminho+da+Ser pente (Esp. 54A-9, par. 1)

Six

The Poetry of Multiple Identities

A feel for language

I am trilingual. My multilingualism could have remained a skill, which then could have led to a career. But I am not trilingual because I thought it would be useful for me to learn German, then French, then finally English. My experience of language reaches deeper than that. Speaking three languages is both part of my identity and a way of life: an entry into the kingdom of words through the music of poetry.

Poetry is one of my favorite forms of communication. Reciting verse is, for me, like learning to play a precious violin and knowing how to improvise in more or less formal situations. It is for that reason that when I am addressing myself to a younger crowd, I encourage them to learn poetry by heart and to entertain a virtually carnal relationship with words. Words don't only have meaning; but a sound, a music that gives meaning a pulse.

Language and poetry invite others to become receptive— it makes them *permeable*. I am struck by what seems to happen to me increasingly often during my appearances nowadays. In fact, it happened to me most recently in Düsseldorf. I was going on about the topic I had been invited to speak on (*Die Empörung*, outrage, etc.) and I was, as usual, elaborating, discussing, and sharing my little stories. I was being asked questions too, but at the end I surprised everyone by announcing that I was going to recite a short poem by Rilke. I have come to develop a style of recitation that incites a certain level of enthusiasm! People like to hear poetry, even poetry that is known to them, and hear it recited in a certain way. This applies too to poetry recited in a completely foreign language. In Frankfurt recently, after a debate with Joschka Fischer which was mediated by Dany Cohn-Bendit, I first addressed a poem in German to the audience, and then the very same poem, but in French, to that same audience. The response to this poem recited in a language no one in the room understood was arresting.

I firmly believe, when communicating a message, that words must carry their degree of meaning; that is undeniable. But you also need intonation, which offers some kind of proof; you need that music and that voice. If I remember correctly, in philosophy's earliest days, certain Ancient Greek philosophers (not only Socrates) would abstain from putting their teachings in writing, preferring instead to relate them in person and to entertain an exchange between writer and reader, rather than tolerate the combined loneliness of both.

Vigor

Of course, there is exhaustion—those train trips and plane trips. But as soon as I find myself in the presence of someone who asks me questions, my desire to answer and to promote my message rekindles the vigor I had thought lost. It's really in my connection with others that I find the vigor to go beyond myself one more time. When I find that I am too absorbed in my readings, I often think that I am lacking some sort of presence, an exchange. It's addictive, you know. There is the audience, you speak, and they burst into applause. It's exhilarating.

Aside from the loud charm of the crowd, certain places help to reinvigorate me. There are first and foremost places where nature rules in its quiet existence. I have the memory of a recent trip to Charité-sur-la-Loire where I was staying in a hotel and where my room had a view on the river on the one side and on a beautiful priory from the 11th Century on the other. The beauty and wonder of those preserved places, where nature and architecture blend without crowding each other, strengthen a little my existing political convictions and specifically, what is most dear to me today: protecting the environment, protecting the earth. That is the impulse behind my involvement with Europe Écologie—Les Verts.

There are also some cities that have been instrumental in the development of my identity and that I hold dear: Berlin, the town of my parents, of my childhood, is one of them. It's stunning to see all of the transformations at work there. It's a completely different city today than the one I knew, and a fascinating city indeed. A few months back I was able, once again, to experience all of its poetry and charm. The WDR channel wanted to interview me at some point during the day, but because of the shenanigans of an Icelandic volcano, their team was unable to make it to Berlin in time; so there I was, in Berlin, free for an entire, beautiful afternoon. The lady who was accompanying me on this trip suggested we take a ride along the Spree. We embarked on one of these *bateaux-mouches,*[66] leaving from the Weidendammer Brücke for an hour-long tour of Berlin: riding toward the old city in one direction, and toward Museum Island, the Reichstag, and, beyond that, toward the brand new government buildings all the way back to the Weidendammer on our way back. I thoroughly enjoyed it. Berlin is probably currently one of the most interesting cities in Europe.

This Berlin has managed to overcome its tormented past. Its renewed architecture, aimed toward the future, doesn't deny anything, but instead integrates its scars into the very fabric of the city. And what hustle and bustle! What cultural vitality! Exhibits, museums, theaters… That city is a concrete utopia where youths from across the world can blend and experience the global community of tomorrow.

---

[66]   Paris river boat; for sightseeing.

I have a peculiar relationship with Berlin and Germany. I believe that the German citizenry is, of all European citizenries, the one that has been the most marked by the twentieth century, and that experienced the twentieth century in its most intense fashion: with greatness and servility, with horror and difficulty, with guilt, with a division and a loss of two historic provinces. They experienced the vilest of atrocities and the most grandiose of victories (Hitler's victories were, at first, literally rousing), and indeed, for your little average German of the time, there was much glory before the horror, the failures, and the destruction.

And yet, beyond all of this bloody tragedy and destruction, the people finally succeeded, in the span of only a few decades, in giving their country a dominant role, in becoming central players in the development of Europe. Executioners to themselves and to others, the German people have, in my opinion, had a unique experience of this entire century and carry with them much of the responsibility of building a better Europe for the twenty-first century.

I am constantly going on about those simple, evident truths on German radio and I'm not sure this message pleases the audience, but I know for a fact that it elicits interest. And I am after all German—not very German anymore, since I am mostly French and nearly as America as European, but I do remain a little German in the soul. As a result, I feel sympathetic toward the fate of those people who have had the courage to face the horrors of the Holocaust and who are now taking charge of identifying those guilty of crimes, who keep the Holocaust alive in their consciences, and who are rebuilding despite it all.

"We are made of such stuff as dreams are made on"

In his very good little book, *Les Identités meurtrières,*[67] Amin Maalouf explains that he always refuses to answer questions about his identity: French, Lebanese, he is all of those and much more, and doesn't want to be pigeonholed in one category, one identity. He's an inspiring example. For my part, it's just as complex. On the one hand, I really feel like a *Berliner Kinder*, the Berlin child, impertinent and mischievous (the German equivalent of the *Gavroche*[68] in some way), and I am certainly more of a *Berliner* than of a *German from Berlin*. Yet, I am also as French as they come. Paris is my city. I am French not only in terms of my nationality but also in my heart. I love France despite all of its faults. And I also love Germany. In fact, might it not be easier to simply consider myself, as Dany Cohn-Bendit once suggested when we were debating those prickly issues of identity, both German and French, and therefore European?

This duality of nationalities came to me in a strange way, without me even realizing it. I arrived in France at the age of seven, in this country that could only be foreign to me. But by the time my preteen years rolled around, when I was perhaps ten or twelve, I was already French: I went to a French *lycée*, I spoke French, my friends were French... I was French. And then, all of a sudden, the government stuck its nose in all of it and I was naturalized French at the age of twenty. I didn't feel any more French for it, or any less

---

[67]   There is one existing translation of this book in English: Maalouf, Amin. *In the Name of Identity: Violence and the Need to Belong.* New York: Arcade, 2001. Print.

[68]   Street urchin in Paris

German for that matter, but I suppose identity papers, like the soil, do not lie.

However, I did immediately experience the utter absurdity of classifications based on nationality: having now become French—and since I had been admitted as a foreign student—I was no longer allowed to attend the École Normale Supérieure. Now French, I had to retake the competitive entrance exam. Given the stringent requirements nowadays, I'm quite certain I wouldn't have succeeded a second time around.

Our identities aren't limited to what appears on our government papers. For instance, I am constantly reminded of that beautiful film that immortalized my mother's life: I am literally the son of *Jules and Jim.*[69] But I'm not sure I have much to say about that whole subject. I don't think our most intimate experiences can ever be fully captured through a medium such as film. Film is a travesty of what we are in reality. I won't accept to be dominated by this portrayal, as moving and famous as it may be.

The ways of identity are complex and subtle. Some things might seem obvious until an event forces you to reconnect with different parts of yourself… According to Maalouf, an identity is not only potentially lethal, but can actually be mutilating. And to limit a person to some arbitrary administrative and bureaucratic categories, as Sarkozy had envisaged, with his ministry of National Identity, is a violation of our intelligence and of our privacy. I won't let a ministry

---

[69] This famous French movie (*Jules and Jim*, 1962) by François Truffaut was based on an eponymous novel by Henri-Pierre Roche, in which the two main characters, Jules and Kathe, were based on Stéphane Hessel's parents (Helen Grund and Franz Hessel).

dictate who I am. My papers don't determine my identity. In fact, Cohn-Bendit doesn't even have French papers, yet who would deny that he is French?

So what state are we in? What are we made of? "Such stuff as dreams are made on" to paraphrase the beautiful Shakespeare quote? The question of identity is very profound. We are living in illogical times in which distances have been dismantled by technology and borders by the scope of the economy. But the condition of the individual in this increasingly disconnected world is delicate. For indeed, in the face of the dissolution of traditional community bonds, whether they are national, religious, or cultural, in the face of the weakening of the 'establishments,' such as the traditional family unit, we are quite bewildered. On the one hand, it is impossible not to view it all as a sort of liberation from the limiting conformism that tradition and religion impose; on another hand, it is hard for all of us to not feel isolated and threatened by this increasingly impersonal and vast world—which is exactly why it can be tempting to boil identities down in such a way.

Yet, no one is ever just "French" or "German." You may in fact feel more belonging to a city or a neighborhood rather than to an actual country; or to a religion, a skin color, a long lost origin, a real or imagined physical place; or perhaps even a sexual orientation, an ideology. Indeed, who should a Turk of Berlin from Kreuzberg who is also a homosexual with leftist tendencies and Sufi sensibilities choose to be? We are all aggregations of different references, sometimes quite contradictory in appearance.

Eureka

Consequently, it is important for us to root ourselves within a community we have chosen. Having fled his own country for France, [Emil] Cioran refused all belonging to a nationality, choosing instead to belong to a language: "One does not inhabit a country; one inhabits a language. That is our country, our fatherland—and no other." Since I speak three languages, I have chosen to have as many home countries as languages I speak—and since two of those languages are spoken globally, my sense of belonging perhaps extends beyond the mere borders of my home nations.

My mention of language's community-building abilities reminds us of this simple idea: No matter what personal liberties we have, no matter how idiosyncratic we all are (sometimes in a more conformist fashion than we like to admit), what matters most is being able to communicate with 'the other,' with others. And this fact reminds me to insist upon another obvious fact: individuals can never be fully disconnected; even when autonomous and independent, the individual can't make it on his own. Man is a social creature.

We all belong to something bigger than ourselves.

I am constantly telling my friends to read this slightly mad but rather beautiful text by Edgar Allan Poe, a text called *Eureka*. It's a text in which Poe attempts to establish a link between the individual and the cosmos: we are in touch with what surrounds us—which ends up isolating us more and more from ourselves—and what surrounds us is of course always part of a larger whole. This attempt at making sense of the universe and of the relation of man to this greater whole rests on a strange axiom: "Because Nothing was, therefore All Things are." But that text offers very beautiful reflections—and reflections of great mystical intensity—on how different realities are intertwined, down from the very specific to the universal.

As it turns out, my mother was the one who made me read that remarkable text; I certainly wouldn't have been as receptive to it without her. Having reread it a few months back, I was very taken once again, even if it doesn't start in the best way. The beginning is somewhat of a joke; it's about a bottle lost at sea. It's not very coherent. The twenty or so pages of the beginning are a little simplistic or silly, since he is not a scientist. But from the moment he launches into this idea of perception of the self and of the cosmos, his message becomes very strong.

One message that is essential to me: individuals are woven into the fabric of something much larger than themselves. Whatever our degree of independence, national or individual, we are most importantly and above all interdependent. I've already alluded to this idea, when addressing Buddhist thought. But it doesn't stop there. We can learn yet more from Buddhist or oriental traditions, in the context of which interdependence has a deeper meaning: we entertain some type of interdependence with all things—living beings, animals, vegetation, and in fact with everything that lives, with all of creation. It's a whole philosophy of continuity and interaction between different elements of the system that considers things more fully than this compartmentalized view we have held for a long time now in the West between what is "us" and "what is not us," between man and nature, between subject and object. In that approach, the usual tendency of holding man apart from all else, of isolating him as though he were a separate entity altogether, is abandoned, since this separation is illusory anyway—even on the level of certain truths we hold fast, such as the separation between the living and the non-living.

After all, there is a kind of dialogical link between all that is. The very definition of living is that death will come and claim you one day; the concept of living carries within it the idea of dying. Jean Claude Carrière plays around with the expression "living God," which, it turns out, is a most absurd oxymoron. Indeed, if God is eternal, he is not "living." Living is the opposite of eternity. If he is God, he is beyond life; as it is indicated in the Sufi tradition, he is "outside of the pages of time."

Divergences of faith

Unlike the French and German ruling majority, I was never a Christian—even out of conformism. In fact, I was first, under my father's influence, interested in the Greek gods. It seemed to me like the notion of the divine could not be entirely embodied by some old man with a beard sitting on his cloud, or by a young man dead on a Roman slave's cross. I preferred the idea of a multiplicity of transcendences: the reign of love where Aphrodite and Eros are nestled; or the reign of art governed by Apollo; the reign of a strange form of justice in which we find Zeus; Ares and his reign of violence, Dionysus and the ecstasy he brings. They are many. They play amongst themselves games to which we must be attentive. And we must respect them all—in particular Hermes, the messenger. I like this idea of a manifold divinity and one in which we aren't exempted of our responsibilities as humans, since Prometheus has done what he needed to so that we may experience our humanity to the fullest.

I have met and often greatly admired many Catholics, Protestants, Orthodox. There were pastors in my family, whom I felt close to and greatly respected in almost all regards—but for one detail, which relates back to my problem with monotheism. Now, careful—I think we must make a difference between monotheism and faith generally: in monotheism there is but one god—the one and only Allah (distinct from the one and only Jehovah), the one and only Christ who is separate from Moses. Such monotheism has fed predictable conflicts for many centuries and has done much harm, much more so than faith as a concept has … well, perhaps not in total numbers, because we are in this modern day, in spite of everything, much more efficient than our ancestors in matters of massacre. I often think of the scale of battles of the past compared to battles today—in the past, all you needed was a captain and a few troops, whose deadly face off would pave the way to peace. Today, before you can achieve peace, at least two million men must be massacred.

And this begs the question, how should we process the absolute horror of the 1940s? During my captivity—at the hands of the Gestapo at Buchenwald and Dora—the belief that helped me endure it all was not one of those monotheist religions (and it wasn't either the faith in the fact that international rights would prevail, which wouldn't have lasted long in the daze of the camps). No, what kept me strong and standing was what had been passed on to me by my family—a perfect example of what essential and useful, necessary things parents can transmit to and teach their children. My parents had given me the Greek Gods on the one hand and poetry on the other. They were both poets and lovers of poetry, and had made me learn poetry by heart from a most tender age. The first poem I ever learned was in English and I learned it without even knowing that language, simply based off of its tonality, its music. It was Poe's little poem "Helen," which is my mother's name.

Poetry for me is "the proof." The proof, out of my personal experiences, that there is a space in which we can freely blossom and no longer find ourselves at the mercy of outside forces with whom we are clashing with, against whom we are fighting. It's a different space altogether. The space provided by art, of course, by the imagination. In other words, a space that does not necessarily connect back to any concrete reality, but goes deeper and puts us in such a position so as to dream: to dream along with the poem, and acquire, through poetry, an increased sense of freedom. It's a feeling I encounter often too in music and in painting.

It seems to me like, in the end, all arts can contribute something to us. I don't think any one of them can claim the right to be the true Universal Art, because our tastes and perceptions naturally cause divergences—even if the reach of certain artists seems to transcend personal preferences, like Mozart, Beethoven, or Piero Della Francesca. Regardless of personal preferences however, I believe that this notion that there must be music, that there must be poetry, is universal. And I have been noticing, much to my delight, that we live in a world that is ever more interconnected in matters of arts, music, painting; I am rather cheered by the idea that art, through this impulse toward beauty we all share, is able to reveal some sort of universality.

Poetry and good fortune

So, when we ask ourselves the questions, *What kind of life is worth living? What kind of life is "good"?* (to revisit Aristotle for a minute), we might answer that one must be responsible and become engaged. Yet, we must also consider the extraordinary scope and importance of the imagination, of art and poetry, without which this effort we make—when we are once again alive, when we are "reborn" after having nearly died—is meaningless. We cannot separate experience from action from meditation.

I started my life by trying to be a philosopher. I had been lucky to have Merleau-Ponty as *Caïman*[70] at the École Normale Supérieure, and I am reminded of all that his

---

[70]   Cayman

great mind bestowed upon me (perhaps even more, on the philosophical level, than my friend Sartre) every time I meet people nowadays who have some interest in philosophy. Good fortune is something with which you live the way you might live with a god; it's a little genie on your shoulder the way you might live with the beyond. It's the attitude that says, *Good things may happen to me and I must endeavor to take advantage of them*. In my case, there was that exceptional instance of being sentenced to death and escaping by taking on the identity of a young Frenchman who himself died of typhus and was sent to the crematorium with my own identity.

It was an extraordinarily important moment. How did I experience it? Each moment of that incarceration I kept in mind the poems my mother had taught me when I was fifteen. That poetry was the best way for me to escape overwhelming sadness and petrifying fear. The question, *What kind of life can and must a man try to live?*, I answered off of my conviction that we only require a certain number of fundamental pillars in our lives: poetry, good fortune, and a taste for 'the other,' meditation, compassion. If you have ever experienced a moment in which these elements come to combine successfully, you will find that it has given each subsequent moment in our life a deeper meaning.

I took this life how it came, with candidness, and with an attitude inherited from my mother. I always speak of her, Helen, as the most important thing that ever happened to me. She told me once, "One must be happy and spread around the happiness one experiences."

In other words, it's by considering yourself happy that you can make others happy and live a happy life. So is happiness something you attract through some kind of force or can you see it coming? Knowing my good fortune, I perhaps tackled certain parts of my life with an attitude of: *You, the one with the good fortune, go for it! You're going to achieve something.* Well, actually, quite often, I didn't end up achieving anything. My life can in no way be considered a string of successes. I've had many failures. I would almost say that, looking back now on my biography, the number of failures is higher than the small number of successes; but I never let myself be destabilized. Failures always seemed necessary in order to go further. And in such cases, resilience—that is to say, the ability to carry on despite it all—served me a lot.

I remember a conversation with Jean-Paul Dollé reaching this conclusion: all said and done, a good life is a life in which self-confidence, despite all of our failures, can build. And it grows stronger yet as it is fed by an emotion sent forth by the imagination. Though our experiences may be tedious, there is always art and poetry as recourse. We only need to recite a line of verse by Baudelaire for everything, all of a sudden, to be alleviated; or we only need to go to Sansepolcro to admire a "Resurrection" by Piero Della Francesca to elevate our souls. Locked, as I was, in the hardworking life of a diplomat with the impossible task to push this or that other tract through, I have always been infatuated with our imaginations.

A sublime courage: the strength of our souls

To understand the soul, I think we should look to sociologist Marcel Mauss's ideas on gift giving in which he elucidates that the true consequence of giving a gift is that this elicits a gift in return or "return gift."[71] It's through the exchange of gifts that you can achieve harmony towards progress. I insist on this word "harmony" because I want to highlight its importance in this ever-growing, ever more fragmented society that seems to have a harder and harder time conceiving of harmonious ways in which we might be able to live together; and this especially in the age of online relationships—even though Sloterdijk is correct to remind us not to underestimate relations created online, because all human relationships develop somewhere in the spectrum that ranges from superficial to deep. I do think however that we have in some ways forgotten how to be together.

Of all the great doctrines that have originated in very different societies over time, but which all share in common that they have endured for thousands of years, we should be able to locate some kind of impulse that would convince us of the fact that we do not need Facebook to instantly reach seven thousand people, an impulse that would teach us instead to feel that friendly ears, willing to help us realize our individual desires into a collective opus, do exist.

---

71   Mauss, Marcel. *The Gift: Forms and Functions of Exchange in Archaic Societies.* New York: Norton, 1967. Print.

This notion of opus is what is most important for each of us. An individual's life itself may be an opus, or that individual may work toward an opus that impacts the lives of others. I believe the impulse exists in all of us; but I also think it can be stifled by two great threats: political repression, which looks to silence the voice of the opposition, and cynicism—of those who need to jealously restrain the creativity of others.

It's against both of those conservative influences that individuals must rise up in order to promote different viewpoints. Individuals, whomever they may be, are never alone, never isolated; they are social, they live with others, and they entertain the ambition of working toward something. "To create is to resist. To resist is to create": this enigmatic saying and its full meaning come to bear in and close my little libel, *Time for Outrage.*

Behind that sententious banality lays the idea that dissatisfaction, indignation, should inspire some sort of resistance against what is causing it. And in order to resist, one must create. Similarly, when individuals feel the need to create, they tend to notice rather quickly that those stifling forces seek to prevent them from doing so and must, as a result, resist those forces—confront them and impose their wills.

Sloterdijk calls it a "production of the self." It is possible that animals engage in it too, but they can only act so far as their instincts will allow them. Man is the animal that has found itself in a position to rise to action, surely thanks to the power of speech, and to create by resisting what prevents him from actualizing his innermost aspirations.

The unity of a man

This thought brings me back to artistic creation, which brings us back to harmony. Harmony occurs when more or less contradictory elements come together to find their balance (like in an orchestra in which the most discordant voices would come together and form a magnificent whole). But we don't get balance initially; first, we get diversity and opposition, and what can emerge from opposition is harmony. It is in surpassing our differences that this marvelous growth we all recognize can occur.

This too applies when considering the unity of a man: man grows and is forged out of the diversity of his passions and contradictory impulses. I think we must view man as a being constantly confronted by both internal and external opposing forces, who is capable of turning this combination into a composition where everything agrees. He does so without renouncing himself, of course—in fact, quite the opposite; by finding within him what can prevail over the two elements that seem to want to destroy each other. In that sense, philosophy is just one of the solutions offered to human beings because, in a certain way, it is a renouncement of action. To exile oneself in wisdom is not changing the world.

Philosophy observes, looks to understand and to know why the world works well or poorly; it provides some ideas on the way in which it could work differently, but its approach remains reserved, distanced. Art consists, on the other hand, in recognizing that reality is diverse, complicated, oppositional, pulsating, sometimes a *Zwickmühle*, a sort of Catch-22, which can only be overcome by creating a different type of reality which agrees better with the soul, which strengthens bonds between all beings.

But what is the soul? The soul is, for me, the tear that runs from my eyes, the tears that run from the eyes of the entire human race. There are some poems I cannot recite without weeping. I discover in them the very emotion of art. In Rilke's "Archaic Torso of Apollo," the poet claims that from such a deep, moving emotion, from such mutilation, a certain strength must emerge.

We are faced with many unsolvable problems today. The question now is whether we will have sufficient confidence in our courage. I believe that is key. It is not enough to remain indifferent; we must keep telling ourselves that what awaits us is not insurmountable, that we have within us sufficiently untapped energies, we must aspire to values that may still seem quite distant. If we can believe the impossible possible, reachable and valuable, we can become makers of harmony.

We have to recognize that, these days, human relations often end poorly. Men, women, children, grandfathers, and great-grandchildren don't always live in harmony. In that respect, we must make a formidable effort so that human beings learn to locate the urge within them to move beyond conflict and toward a deeper understanding of each other, and therefore toward compassion for each other. We need to infuse those high moral values with the same kind of appeal that draws people to invest in the Stock Market. It's more profitable in the long run anyway!

Passionate love is a magnificent investment. Anyone who has ever felt the rapture of great love will know what I am speaking of—and this, even when it is not reciprocated. I must confess to entertaining a fair amount of doubt on reciprocated love. I think that, too often, it's an excuse to contain passion. Maintaining that idealized version of the other you met at first glance is the true task. I'd like to look to the recent revival of asceticism, thanks to Peter Sloterdijk's latest book. I immediately opened my dictionary to find the meaning in French of the word *ascèse*[72]: it's a practice that rejects the limits we usually impose on action. And, as such, I think it's a practice that conceives very well of ways in which man is able to surpass himself. The term originates with the athletes from the Antiquity. At first, it meant nothing more than "training," but training is already a movement toward the improbable. Sloterdijk makes note of the fact that sport as observed in Classical Antiquity brings proof that the feats of a few never remain meaningless to those who are observing. Even if these observers are aware of the fact that they would not be able to reproduce what they have just witnessed, they are nonetheless deeply moved. The acrobatic feats we witness in athletics carry an anthropological significance immediately recognized by the observers, for they under-stand that it concerns them too, that human beings can outdo themselves when they make an effort.

Today, we are witnessing a crisis in role models in society. Sports are corrupted by money, but the crisis extends also

---

[72]   Asceticism

to painting and to some other fields. The function of role models must remain more or less intact, for they play a part in the handing down of art and industry. Art and industry are still effectively handed down, but in many cases the place formerly occupied by our role models is uncertain and damaged. And they become a source of discouragement. People don't understand anymore from where to draw their direction, a direction that usually arises from wanting to acquire a certain virtue.

I share Sloterdijk's concern in the matter. It seems obvious to me that, especially as concerns political leadership, this crisis of role models deepens from year to year. And the slow march to the French elections of 2012 have not really triumphed over my concerns; actually, quite the opposite. The crisis of role models is an ethical problem.

The ethic of dreams

The final volume of *La Méthode* by Edgar Morin is titled "Ethics." Ethics: what a marvelous word. But like all magical words, it can sometimes have a hidden meaning. It must be considered carefully. Once again, we return to Aristotle: ethics are distinguished from morals which relate, instead, to certain conventions adopted by this or that society at a given time (a code of conduct, in some way, which indicates how one must behave). Society defines its moral code. We may therefore speak out, with a little belligerence, or at least with some level of criticism, against often-hypocritical Bourgeois or conformist morals. Ethics however, is something entirely different. We could say that a moral code is public, whereas ethics are personal.

Ethics are defined by a given situation; it's doing the right thing at the right moment. We also come across that concept quite a bit in Plato's *Republic*, which concerns itself with "justice," and we even find it in the Hindu notion of *dharma*. An action that is right is true and not only by its very nature, but based on the person performing the act and the situation in which the person is called to react.

Ethics are therefore rooted in our reactions to reality. Those reactions can be sorted in different categories based on whether their intent is toward self-aggrandization, individualism, which is to be expected and understandable; whether their intent is to benefit those whom we love; or, whether their intent results from a desire to benefit the greatest number of individuals. There is, somewhere in Montesquieu's *Spirit of Laws,* a lovely passage on the relationship between different interests that apexes with the interests of humanity as a whole. I'd like to make it clear that I firmly believe in this idea of a greater good for humanity, and in the fact that there exists, globally, a sense of what is good and what is bad. And it is around that particular idea that we must build a corpus of universal values.

My good fortune—to have survived those horrors, to have been there and associated with the writing of this decisive text[73] destined to give shape to this corpus of values, to have infused it with necessary clarity, readability so that

---

[73]   The Universal Declaration of Human Rights

it could be accepted by all doubtless, founds my unshakable conviction that human societies have a beautiful future ahead of them.

The twelve writers took three years—from 1945 to 1948—to agree on the freedoms and rights that the Declaration should define and to certify, above all, its universality, which was unique in the history of international texts. It was in no way, however, the formulation of a moral code present, at the time, in Western societies and democracies with little consideration for the East. No. The ambition was a larger one. Ethics are at the heart of the Universal Declaration of Human Rights. And this is where I draw my optimism from. I believe in the progress of humanity, as contradictory as its stages may be. I believe in it, with its advances, its setbacks, its collective pushes and individual breakthroughs.

I, the Westerner, the Cartesian, forged in Greek and German philosophy, agnostic and rational, entertain a true curiosity toward Buddhism. First of all, because it is not monotheistic and because I am an obstinate opponent of monotheism. When people ask me how I live without God, I answer, in a swell of provocative pride, that I do just fine on my own. But what I like about the Buddhists is the instilling of this sort of awakening of consciousness through exercises in which body and soul are connected. I therefore believe that we could try—not necessarily by all becoming Buddhists; but by thinking the way they do—to tackle serious problems that face us by adopting an attitude that says, *Here is how we, we who are not yet in power, we who are not yet in possession of significant financial means (but who, little by little, will grow in influence), can try to answer our problems: here are some values upon which we can all unanimously, universally agree.* I look to return the world to men in some way.

When I am thrown that typical realist's objection, when I am dubbed a sweet dreamer, I do confess to sometimes being embarrassed. It's an objection that is not easy to counter. The state of things is sufficiently depressing to make us lose all faith, all hope; but that's why it's interesting to be very old and to be able to tell yourself, with the wisdom conferred by your age, that there have been times in which things were much worse and that those horrendous things ended up being resolved. Take Europe, for instance. The building of the European Union and the institutions of the EU have become recurring subjects of more or less factual political attacks. Yet, when you think about it, since 1957, and particularly since 1989, all Europeans (with the exception of the Balkans), and also the Russians for the most part, have been living together, in some state of peace. It is impossible not to view this as progress when you compare it to the history of the eighteenth or nineteenth centuries—or even the twentieth century.

Old age offers at least this amount of perspective: you are able to put bad things into perspective by looking back at all of the obstacles you have already crossed. There is no logical reason for this natural progression of things to now be interrupted. After all, there was Hiroshima and Auschwitz, then the failure of Copenhagen. The half-failures of Cancun are certainly serious and disappointing; but they do leave room for some hope. For indeed, we know now why it's serious and how to change things.

I shall return now to the notion of "ethics:" if we are conscious of the importance of those values we claim to carry forth, and we believe that we can have some impact because we are in contact with a larger and larger number of the earth's men and women, we cannot possibly despair. Naturally, there will always be limitations, but limitations are merely to be moved past and to become places of transition. And if so many limitations turn into doors we must push open, then maybe, with those values of justice and tolerance, we will push through them and we will arrive at a "collective of human societies" which will agree on what is indispensable to implement. And we will do all of this together because each member of this collective will understand that it is necessary, and, indeed, it will be universally recognized—that our survival on earth depends upon our mutual understanding of each other, and that our lives are made the better for it. Is this some dreamy utopia? Maybe... But can we not believe that one day Eros will vanquish Thanatos?

Hyperion's Song of Fate[74]

You walk above in the light,
Weightless tread a soft floor, blessed genii!
Radiant the gods' mild breezes
Gently play on you
As the girl artist's fingers
On holy strings.

Fateless the heavenly breathe
Like an unweaned infant asleep;
Chastely preserved
In modest bud,
For ever their minds,
Are in flower
And their blissful eyes
Eternally tranquil gaze,
Eternally clear.

But we are fated
To find no foothold, no rest,
And suffering mortals
Dwindle and fall
Headlong from one
Hour to the next,
Hurled like water
From ledge to ledge
Downward for years to the vague abyss.

---

[74]   Hölderlin, Friedrich. *Selected Poems and Fragments*. Trans. Michael Hamburger. Ed. Jeremy D. Adler. London: Penguin, 1998. 25-27. Print.

Seven

Learning to Become Engaged

The essence of a leader

Becoming engaged is not an innate behavior. To stay clear of all engagement, to keep our private lives protected from what could upend them, represents a constant temptation that becomes nearly irresistible when we are continually subject to skepticism, or even scorn and anger, toward political parties and national or international groups. Moving beyond that initial impulse is only possible once we have acquired a philosophy rooted in knowledge of history and considered what those who have lived through it have to say.

When we old buggers demand of you to become engaged, it is our duty too to first remind you that no change in the functioning of our societies was ever attained without a certain level of engagement from the citizens.

In certain instances, a single man or a woman, defined by their courage and lucidity, was sufficient to inspire faith that this or that battle was not lost: Jeanne d'Arc for France, for instance, who was handed over to The House of *Plantagenet*, and de Gaulle for Europe, which had been handed over to the Nazis.

More often than not however, it is only the converging of concurring minds that make us move forward. Certain of those minds happen to be better organized than others. Find those you trust today and contribute your energy, your dynamism, to them. Help them, in the process, upend this pitiful state of affairs.

In Amin Maalouf's fascinating essay "Le Dérèglement du monde,"[75] there is a very pertinent passage on the "lost legitimacy" of different political regimes, whether they were autocratic and despotic or democratic and liberal. I think legitimacy is not sacrosanct; it is justified and unjustified in turn, depending on leaders and the conditions in which it originates.

The key to power in this contemporary world rests within this question of legitimacy—whether power is acquired through the show of strength and the imposition of fear, or through wealth and influence, or is acquired by

---

[75]   "Dissolution of World Orders." More information can be found here: http://www.eutopiainstitute.org/2010/10/amin-maalouf-the-dissolution-of-world-orders/

a constitutional state or a democracy. Each regime finds different motivations behind its desire for power within certain given historic and social conditions. Democracy is making slow progress and all those other regimes are far from reaching their end.

Illegitimacy feeds a deaf and diffuse anguish, which may translate into revolts: a healthy revolt infatuated with freedom, such as the ones rocking the Arab world, or a bitter revolt infused with populist resentment, such as the ones in our own parts. I believe that the feeling of having lost our bearings and our way, which pervades the world today, is linked to the feeling that we are not being led correctly. Forgive me for repeating this little exercise in admiration, but I must once again sing the praises of that fractious and anarchist friend of mine, who so rebels against propriety and certain responsibilities.

It is a well-known fact that I have a great deal of respect for Dany Cohn-Bendit because he is someone who has been known, in important moments, historic moments as they say, to find the right and relevant words. A good leader is recognized by his or her ability to make sense of a situation in a moment when those present are willing to listen. We must "make sense" of things, as the Anglo-Saxons put it; that is to say, ask crucial questions and bring pieces of the answers. This does not preclude us from making errors in judgment or failing to consider certain things due to given time-pressures. I am certain that some choices, which seem pertinent at the time of the decision, will reveal themselves to be worse than we thought. We certainly all applauded after the agreements in Dayton, which didn't solve anything in the long run and even provided grounds for the ethnic partitioning of Bosnia… but the massacre had to be stopped!

That said, mistakes and all, the essence of a leader is found in this ability to make light of the world, of a situation, to illuminate us when we are at a crossroad, to identify our goals: *We must go toward that, in this way.* When Emmanuel Kant claims that man needs a master, he doesn't mean that people are calves or sheep without autonomy or a critical mind—he is simply reminding us of the mystery of political power, of the right kind of power, which can withstand the tension between the universal values which must inspire it and the selfish tendencies of each individual. He reminds us that the fundamental mission of any mentor is teaching emancipation, both at school and in politics.

A certain mediocrity found nowadays tends to result in an increased number of individuals quarreling over their specific interests as opposed to holding actual discussions on the stakes and purpose of our existence. In his essay *La Mobilisation infinie,*[76] Sloterdijk pronounces this very severe judgment on the political characters of our time: "Based on my latest analyses, it is pointless to question whether this or that politician has the fiber of a commander in chief; or if he belongs to this or that party; or if the interests of the taxpayers are, in his mind, above financial gain; or if his values have been acquired through contact with men of good will and synodal congregations; or if he fights over his wallet

---

[76] Sloterdijk, Peter. *La Mobilisation infinie: vers une critique de la cinétique politique.* Paris: C. Bourgois, 2000. Print.

with prostitutes in front of a hotel in New York. Those are all insignificant sins or secondary virtues. *What is paramount is to know whether he prides himself on having an in-depth awareness of the problems we are currently facing.*"

Someone like Dany has always been capable of designating the objective and the way with a reasonable degree of optimism, and his words ring true. His lucidity requires him to recognize when something is poorly set up, and, like me, he worries rightly about the unhealthy trends at work in Europe today. But he never gives up and he believes that if things aren't going well, then it means they can go better! As long as… His engagement is optimistic and ready to take a chance on the improbable, on the tremors and borrowed time that bind us all.

Modest as he is, he would say that the historical conditions of our respective engagements were different—it is true that June '40 and May '68 cannot be compared. But that does not diminish the importance of any engagement in our history.

By force of circumstance:
being in the world inside the current of history

Losing others is the worst thing I have ever experienced. Thirty-six of us came to Buchenwald. Of those thirty-six, sixteen were hung and fourteen were shot. Only three were saved. I did not feel despair—that's not the right word—rather dejection in the face of everything that took place, which was truly scandalous and unbearable. Indignation was the notion I believed could most readily go up against all that was going wrong, and, it seemed to me, the best message I could transmit to those who wonder what to do with their lives—an essential question indeed. Life must serve some purpose, and it can serve many agreeable purposes like love, poetry, our imagination, but it must also serve to resist what makes us outraged.

I am invited to high schools to speak of the Universal Declaration of Human Rights since I am credited as having played an essential role in the design of that founding text… It is, actually, quite exaggerated. I was only a young diplomat, a recent graduate of the *Concours du Quai d'Orsay*,[77] recruited by the United Nations to take my place alongside some very important people such as René Cassin, Eleanor Roosevelt, and Charles Malik, who were all working towards drafting the text. But I was there, and I experienced in person the building of those universal values. I derived wondrous moral and intellectual benefits from the experience. To participate in this reflection on established, fundamental liberties, on civil, economic, and social rights, which we all deserve, does provide you with quite a foundation! And it seems to me that a young man who is not conscious of the existence of such values and of their desecration a bit everywhere in the world, including within his own country—whatever

---

[77] Though a geographical spot in Paris, when referred to with a capital "Q," the Quai d'Orsay is taken to mean the seat of the French Ministry of Foreign Affairs. From *Le Grand Robert & Collins:* "In French towns, the word **quai** refers to a street running along the river, and appears in the street name itself. In Paris, some of these street names are used by extension to refer to the famous institutions situated there: the **Quai Conti** refers to the Académie française, the **Quai des Orfèvres** to the headquarters of the police force, and the **Quai d'Orsay** to the Foreign Office." The ENS (école Normale Supérieure) and the Quai d'Orsay work closely together to instruct students in diplomacy (geography department). The "Concours" of the Quai d'Orsay refers to a competitive examination taken at the end of one's studies.

country he may be from—well, if he does not have that kind of stimulation in his life, he is missing out on a large portion of what makes up the joy of living.

I believe we are happy in life when we are engaged.

Is it even possible to live life without being engaged? Engagement is a form of reaction to history—like Zola who refuses the sacrifice of an innocent to honor the nation; or Jean Moulin and those first Frenchmen who proceeded to London from June 1940 on; or [Bronisław] Geremek who remained in Gdansk in 1980 when [Lech] Wałęsa had asked him to. But the price to pay is often forsaking yourself, and, in a lot of cases, the end of peace of mind, the loss of your personal freedoms, and sometimes even suffering or death.

I've also had the temptation of disengagement. After the Resistance; the trials of the camps; the maelstrom of the founding of the UN; after five years at the United Nations as a young international official where I was involved with marvelous things such as the establishment of world organizations for health, work, refugees, education, science, and culture, I've nonetheless sometimes wanted to have a different life, to come back to France, to leave New York where I was slowly saturating. I even thought of following in the path of my writer parents, of trying to write. I took up my pen and began to write what would be a masterpiece that would change the world's predicament: *La Société du vouloir-faire.*[78]

---

[78]   Translates to "The Society of Willed Doing"

That phase lasted three months: long enough for me to notice that the text was worth nothing and that I would be better off returning to work for the United Nations, which itself resulted in, a few years later, my collaboration with Pierre Mendès France, on the matter of Indochina, specifically.

Since then, I've never again had this desire to withdraw, which can grip us after such trials, or the desire to avail myself of anything in honor of the pursuit of my own personal fantasies. I must admit that if I did not pursue this venture, I could have tried to improve the beginning of that text—it is because I felt that I was not made to be an essayist or a writer. So I worked myself back into the fold, back into this little routine where you write reports to the minister telling him, "I believe it is indispensable for us to now…" And the minister reads your reports with great kindness and even pays you a compliment now and then, telling you, "Your report was very interesting indeed, so I put it in the left drawer instead of the right one."

Since then, I have turned from a diplomat into a militant for a certain idea of justice and human rights: a shift from political engagement through diplomacy to political engagement in society through society. At this moment in my life, like anyone who has aged a lot, I am no longer charged with a career or a function. My last function was to represent France at the conference on Human Rights in Vienna in 1993, at the crux of the Balkan war. It was a terrible time and was my final act as an official. Since then, I have only represented myself and, as a result, tend to pour my energy into causes.

With all required modesty, I see myself a little bit in Sartre's heritage. What I admired so much in him was that, from a certain point of view, he didn't make too much of a difference between "good" and "bad" causes. It's a cause; therefore it must be defended. I am sometimes caught, these days, like Sartre, in a similar trap.

There are three ways for a man to concern himself with his future

Let's come back for a minute to this failed writer experience. I was thirty-two. I had just left my position at the United Nations and, in those three quiet months that lay ahead, I told myself that I had to write. The experience I'd had up until then was that of an environment that seemed accessible to all people and all nations. It's what Roosevelt had wanted: to form a large organization in which everyone was represented. My ambition was to reflect upon what that 'world society' could become.

There are three ways for a human being to find a purpose, to do what Sloterdijk calls in *Tu dois changer ta vie*: "the human exercise" (meaning "the production of man through himself").[79] At the time, I gave a very pragmatic account of it by identifying three forms of desire: there is the desire to be, the desire to have and the desire to do. The desire to be corresponds for me to that period of time when

---

[79] Sloterdijk, Peter. *"Du Mußt Dein Leben Ändern": Über Religion, Artistik Und Anthropotechnik*. Frankfurt Am Main: Suhrkamp, 2009. Print. Title translates most literally to "You Must Change Your Life."

one had to be noble to "be;" your birth and heritage defined your essence. But that period ended with the French revolution. Then came a Bourgeois period in which everything was defined by "having." *The idea was, I am someone because I have my house, my trade, my wife, my money, my capital...* but that approach also realized its limits with the horrendous crisis of 1929. I thought, therefore, that we needed to find something new, something that I wanted to call the "Society of Willed Doing." We'd have an environment within which individuals would choose to outdo themselves, to find themselves through what they do. And, of course, if they know how to create, if they become artists, then they would go where the "doing" was most needed.

I got through a hundred or so pages which were worth nothing and which I threw out immediately. Yet, since then, I've never stopped pondering that reflection: it must be possible to understand our essence, the nature of what we are building through this global society. This phenomenon is complex. We could quite easily cave in to the temptation of dialectical action, the way Hegel does, in which we'd move from the particular to the universal, from the local to the national, from the national to the global.

Today there's a grain of sand stuck in the system; there's a jam from which we can't move forward, a jam only citizens can begin to unclog. In this repetitive game of three, where political power, financial and economic pressures, and citizens (who are both the purpose and at the root of the other two) attempt to achieve a balance as best they can, it is the latter who retain the key to this equation that neither governments nor economic powers are in any position to resolve. Under the weight of political decisions, which themselves are bound to economic pressure, the citizen is in truth the only lever, the heart of the system, who can still act according to his will. He only needs to react, to become aware of his power to find the foundations for public action within him. He should remember, along with La Boétie, that he is only obeying the forces that act upon him because he is willing to—that his life of bondage is voluntary. The reasoning is then very simple: to flip the triangle over to place the citizen at the top. To make sure the forces that act upon him are at his service and not the opposite. That is what pushed me to bring that old notion of indignation back into fashion.

Sloterdijk did me the honor and kindness of using my little bestseller to develop an original perspective of history. He indeed considers that the origins of indignation go back to a time when the disappointment of citizens toward their own homeland truly began. According to him, we can claim that philosophy herself is the daughter of indignation, of that disappointment. After a Peloponnesian war of thirty years between Sparta and Athens, the citizens of Athens had lost faith in their political community. And it's the same impulse that led philosophy to be engendered—as a result of a spiritual rift with the political community that had so brutally betrayed promises of happiness, justice, and peace. Since that point in time, the history of ideas in Europe would forever be the result of a disappointment more than two thousand years old. In the end, indignation, and the impulse to be outraged, would inscribe themselves in the great current of disappointment of human beings tired of having to take part in a community that is ignoble—meaning "non noble." There is a certain notion of "recovery of pride" in the act of becoming outraged. The notion of dignity is at the root of the world "indignation," for the one who becomes indignant, outraged, is looking to remember a long lost dignity. The act of outrage helps him reinstate his memory of it.

But all of this goes much deeper. It's interesting to note that indignation can correspond to a metamorphosis or a political alchemy which produces a noble reaction (the fight, engagement), which itself springs forth from a much less noble raw material (resentment, anger).

For Sloterdijk, this call to indignation is essential because it offers to elevate this "alchemical reaction" toward freer, more dignified, more noble actions, which rises above the level of what initially caused them. For it would be very dangerous to unleash those energies in their raw state. They must be transcended.

As for my part, in reading Sloterdijk, I rediscovered what an important foundation Antiquity provided in the development of our universal—and finally eternal—values. Those values have undergone many transformations over the course of history, in some cases advances, in others regressions, but either way they constitute a base solid enough for us to press up against them and prop ourselves up in order to hold our heads high. In Plato, in Aristotle and, in my mind, maybe even more so in Heraclitus and Parmenides, we encounter the foundations of contemporary thought

imperative to understanding life and the world, foundations I called upon at two crucial moments of my existence:
during the Resistance and then at the United Nations, in
drafting the Universal Declaration, and, in particular in the
very first article, which I always quote *in extenso*, so fundamental does it seem to me: "All human beings are born free
and equal in dignity and rights. They are endowed with reason and conscience and should act towards one another in
a spirit of brotherhood."

Therein is captured the essence of what a citizen is.
A citizen is someone who has fundamental rights that must
be protected by political powers—in other words, by governments. When governments fail in their mission, the citizen has a right and a duty to protest. A citizen is, of course,
correct to fight; but above all, he or she must recover his dignity through indignation.

This is only a summary, of course. Sloterdijk actually
reminds us of it, but the classical foundations of European
thought have gone through many changes to reach their
contemporary state. In fact, he adds, the principal inten-
tion of philosophy in the Antiquity was less so participation in political life than withdrawal. Because philosophy
is in some way the daughter of failure and disappointment,
she cannot conceive of the possibility of an honest and
reasonable man's willingness to integrate into the current
community. Then, for two thousand years, we saw some
regression—since back in the time of monarchy there was
less of a need for philosophers than for religious leaders.
Rejected by the religious intelligentsia, philosophy was

only to return after the French Revolution to "interpret, this time, our contemporary disappointments." In the end, the biggest difference between the Moderns and the Ancients is a rejection of resignation. Antiquity endured in a balance of wisdom and resignation. But the Moderns do not have the same relationship with disappointment. Their reflex is: *What could be different could be better...* Disappointment, therefore, becomes a driving force, stimulating a movement toward a better future. It is, as a matter of fact, the subject of Ernst Bloch's important book: *Le Principe espérance.*[80]

The danger is: if the power that moves us cannot succeed in changing the state in which we live, we might fall back into disappointment and lock ourselves inside religion again. It's what could have happened at different times in our recent history. But at present, under the pressure of a crisis that is becoming global, it is possible and urgent for us to reconnect with the philosophical tradition that acknowledges that things cannot go on and that "you must change your life."

The rights of "the other": the challenge of interdependence

The multifaceted crisis that we are going through is deep, brutal, and dangerous. But, as Edgar Morin always smartly reminds us, crises are precisely moments in which our

---

[80]   An English translation of Ernst Bloch's *Das Prinzip Hoffnung* is available: Bloch, Ernst. *The Principle of Hope.* Cambridge, MA: MIT, 1986. Print.

awareness of danger helps us uncover paths to salvation. Surely, the crisis provides us with an opportunity for a broad rise in awareness. Men and women, in the West, though not only there, can gain awareness that the exercise of "being" human can overcome certain terrible burdens like the desire for possession and competition. Perhaps my great age provides me with some detachment, yet I remain convinced that we should all possess the least amount possible, only what we need to satisfy our needs, and that we should not be exceptional, only strong, and helpful toward all. The challenge of our times is perhaps simply to accept our conditions of interdependence and solidarity with nine billion other people; quite a steep number.

The challenge is there: to think and live in an astonishing coexistence with the rest of the human race. It's true that this situation is very new. For the first time in history, the word humanity is not abstract. The concept has become a terrifying reality because no one knows how we can live with nine billion neighbors, and on a single Earth. For it is not only a unanimous life with other men we must envisage; we must now also accept our condition of co-citizenry with an entire system of living beings: animals, plants, complex organisms, and ecosystems... "Humans and non-humans form a new global assembly which needs its own constitution," Sloterdijk jokes. I must confess that the idea of having to draft a sort of new Universal Declaration of the Rights of Humans in Nature and their Environment, enthuses me as much as it worries me, so titanic does the task seem.

But my meetings with the editor of *Time for Outrage*, Sylvie Crossman, who is blessed with a very deep and personally-felt knowledge of ancient human groups and their experiences, reassured me. How, for instance, did they go about preserving their close relationships with their natural environment? We find answers not only in the Dalai Lama's message, his tireless effort to keep this natural ease at play between man and nature from wasting away, but also in the attitude of the Aborigines of Australia, the Navajo Indians, and the Indians from the Amazon and Peru, and their approach which integrates society and the ground from whence we originate. They have shown themselves able to maintain an equilibrium, which has allowed them to endure and preserve a certain mutual consideration amongst individuals, hierarchical systems accepted by all, a very strong bond with nature--forming in the end a whole we could call harmonious, a whole in which, based on established rules, those who rupture that equilibrium or violate its harmony must be punished.

But considering the types of lives we have developed, our model of civilization looks more like fireworks than a balanced system. Spending, wasting, Sloterdijk suspects that there exists another unspoken right which is implied by our "human rights": the right to waste, the right to take part in the fireworks, in the hunt for happiness, in the great race against time during which we try to maximize our enjoyment.

Consider the notion of work. I remember this book by André Gorz, *Métamorphoses du travail*,[81] which had marked

---

[81]   Gorz, André. *Métamorphoses du travail: critique de la raison économique.* Paris: Gallimard, 2004. Print.

me, so well did it confirm the flaws in our attitude toward the essence of life by exposing the flaws in our attitude toward work. It was quite close to what Edgar Morin describes in his books: What do we know about man after all? Is he, in the end, a diligent creature who must work, get excited, love, and think? Or is he? He is indeed required to do all of those things, so how should he go about arranging those often contradictory but unavoidable activities into a harmonious whole? How should we foster in each of us the poet, the worker, the street acrobat, the builder, the philosopher, and the citizen?

This reflection on the disproportionate place that work occupies and the constraints it imposes upon us, and for which we are compensated only by the ability to become consumers (another injunction), is also very well developed by Ivan Illich and Herbert Marcuse—so many reflections that might have prevented the disaster in which we live today. Reflections on the functioning of the economy were inseparable from the thinking of the Left—in France namely, where the Left has spent its time trying to protect the rights of workers, to spread the wealth, etc. Time and again however, the Left locked itself into an essentially Marxist system.

By refusing that paid work be the basis of the system, Gorz, Illich, and Marcuse offer solutions that move us beyond the Marxist impasse. They are only now starting to be understood. Illich wanted, for instance, for mandatory work to be reduced a maximum while creative work would be increased a maximum. He believed this would give rise to a happier society. Gorz offered a more solid reasoning because he did not deny the necessity of the market or of paid work, but proposed instead a more just allocation of jobs so that work might transform into an occupation in which creativity would play an integral role.

The fireworks of abundance, of which Sloterdijk speaks, rest on this connection between paid work and unrestrained compensatory consumption. In order to solve the equation of our contemporary world, we will have to resume our reflections at the time when economic reform and reform of thought occur. The numbers are staggering. We would need two planets for nine billion people to live the European way and five for them to live the American way... it's literally, mathematically, and economically unsustainable. Yet, I don't see many "reasonable" people filling the posts of ministers and other government posts worrying about it a great deal—save Michel Rocard, who is no longer in power, and the ecologists, who struggle to be heard.

It's clear that we can no longer limit ourselves to a purely Western interpretation of human rights; that is to say, an exponential, maximalist version. There are lessons to be learned from the wisdom of other civilizations, which must force us to revisit our established survival code. As Sloterdijk puts it, one of the major challenges of our present century is without a doubt "to develop a form of civilization in which the force of Western culture would be subdued." Edgar Morin speaks, to his end, of a "politics of civilization" in which we would look to keep the best from our past while correcting the deep-rooted imbalances of our outlook on the world, nature, and ourselves.

The effort to fight the dangers that face us today resides in how we use the resources of vitality that exist in each of us. Does it not? Morin repeats it: we need a reform of thought and lifestyle that would prime us for a full-scale societal and economic reform. We must ponder the issue in these terms: do we have within ourselves a will that can be put into action; a will, which might, up until now, have been overshadowed by our desire, above all, to always earn more, which might have been overshadowed by this *hybric* imagination (meaning, an imagination "marked by a hubris") which goes against harmony?

Fate is back

The following took place during a dinner in Paris with a few friends. I left for a few minutes and, as I returned to my seat, I was told, "Peter just declared that fate is back." I was perplexed. What did Sloterdijk mean by this strong statement? And suddenly he launched into the following explanation: "We have entered the era of the second doomsday. The incontrollable is back, now more than ever." It's fascinating that, after two centuries spent in our conviction that man is the master of his destiny, that he controls the powers that act upon him, this notion of fate resurfaces. Is this the a relief of a curse? We could feel rather relieved, reveling in the idea that there exists an authority greater than ourselves influencing our ability to reach what we desire.

Leibniz spoke with certain contempt of the *destin à la turque*[82]; for him, fatalism was a crime against human freedom. And what of all of the thinkers of the Enlightenment? It seemed clear that progress was nothing more than a succession of acts of sabotage against fate. Fate had to be sabotaged. Is there a connection with religion? In the camps, we always referred to those who seemed unlikely to survive as "Muslims." They would walk around the camps dejected, like the living dead. Their hope was gone. Our expression arose from the popular misconception that Islam is a religion of fate, a fatalistic religion, which is, of course, a complete exaggeration, as is almost everything that is said about religions generally.

But there does exist a genuine Muslim version of the Western *fatum*: the Turkish *kismet*, a poetic and splendid word that literally signifies "written," Sloterdijk reminded us. The notion *fatum* applies to what has been *said*; whereas the *kismet* applies to what has been *written*—what is written is symbolically equivalent to being predestined for Muslims.

Thankfully, the culturalist's perspective does not disregard the relevance of the Arab Spring in 2011. We can quote *Lawrence of Arabia* and that moment when somebody should have been sentenced to death and has opposed himself to it, exclaiming triumphantly, "Nothing was written!" But in an ironic twist of fate in the movie's plot, that very same character is killed at the next opportunity and so the

---

[82]   Hessel may be referring to the *Fatum Mahumetanum* by Leibniz. More information in "The Fatum Mahumetanum" (http://unesdoc.unesco.org/images/0019/001917/191745e.pdf. on page 252).

fatum is fulfilled. It's the same sad story as the Sufi tale of Samarkand's *rendezvous* with Death, or of Oedipus trying to evade his destiny. Greek mythology, too, demonstrates that what we attempt to escape eventually catches up with us.

> The Appointment at Samarra: One day, the servant of the grand Vizir came to find him and told him, "Master, I was at the market and I met Death there; she came towards me and I was so afraid that I have decided to leave this town for Samarra." The grand Vizir heads to the market and meets Death there, whom he reprimands for having scared his servant into fleeing elsewhere. Death answers the grand Vizir, "When I approached your servant, it was simply to tell him that I was thinking of finding him, tonight, in Samarra."[83]

According to Sloterdijk, *Fate is back*—meaning some power that pushes us to renounce our ability to act is upon us once more, is replacing willpower with powerless wills. Nietzsche is not too far off. He had already brought

---

[83] That same story was retold in 1933 by W. Somerset Maugham: "There was a merchant in Bagdad who sent his servant to market to buy provisions and in a little while the servant came back, white and trembling, and said, Master, just now when I was in the marketplace I was jostled by a woman in the crowd and when I turned I saw it was Death that jostled me. She looked at me and made a threatening gesture. Now lend me your horse, and I will ride away from this city and avoid my fate. I will go to Samarra and there Death will not find me. The merchant lent him his horse, and the servant mounted it, and he dug his spurs in its flanks and as fast as the horse could gallop he went. Then the merchant went down to the marketplace and he saw me standing in the crowd and he came to me and said, 'Why did you make a threating gesture to my servant when you saw him this morning?' 'That was not a threatening gesture,' I said. 'It was only a start of surprise. I was astonished to see him in Bagdad, for I had an appointment with him tonight in Samarra.'"

to light the notion of climbing and falling wills. There is a great fatalistic vein within human beings that senses, nearly triumphantly, that nothing can be done. In the face of the intangible yet all-too-real forces that act upon us—whether financial, economic, climatic, or even political—it would seem that it is impossible to control, despite the existence of democracy or our mobilized neighbors down the street, this temptation to give up, which is very strong indeed. And, then, consequently, political action merely turns into attempts at preserving the *status quo*. The fact that any idea of progress makes us shudder is a victory for the dedicated conservative.

The art of embracing the unknown

Sabotaging destiny, keeping it from becoming actualized against our will, breaking with the *status quo*—when engaging ourselves, we must accept the risk of moving past the nuances and complexities of a given situation in favor of action. There is a price to pay for simplifying things, for approaching reality clear of contingencies. Edgar Morin taught me that nothing is simple. But it seems to me that even complex things may be approached in a simpler way. A character like Cohn-Bendit embodies the ability to surpass those complexities which so often paralyze us in the decision-making process. He recognizes all of the issues at hand, takes them into account, but then, at a certain point, endowed with intuition, reflection, and responsibility, he is capable, despite his doubts, to devise some sort of solution—a more or less complex and sophisticated one, but one with a clearly marked objective.

It's what I personally attempted in a different context (only I am not a 'politician' in the literal sense of the term). I am fully conscious, however, of the strong need for clear and positive messages. Simple does not mean simplistic.

The example of the debates on whether or not we must support the revolution against Gaddafi in Libya illustrates this idea that we must look beyond certain complexities to make the most meaningful choice, rather than allowing ourselves to be paralyzed by the details. Who cares if we do not know much about the rebels, their origins, or their long-term objectives? In Cohn-Bendit's view, in the case of 'new' Tunisia and the European Parliament[84] for instance, "Realpolitik calls for us to entirely support the ambition of Arab populations toward freedom and democracy." Who cares if they are now more or less in tune with our Western interests—and, as a matter of fact, what exactly are those interests? Oil? Immigration? Is it the fight against terrorism? Who cares if those new leaders were not elected? In the fight against a tyrant, do they not represent a legitimate option? After all, de Gaulle and Jean Moulin were not any more elected than they, and yet, for a large majority of the French people, they embodied an idea of France, a legitimacy that the legal government of Vichy no longer embodied. So, again, who cares?

---

[84]   In January 2011, the European Parliament offered its full support "in view of a democratic transition" to Tunisia, which was, at the time, in the midst of turmoil.

We cannot *not* recognize the Interim Libyan National Transitional Council, especially in view of the imbalance between Gaddafi's armed forces—his weapons, his tanks, his mercenaries—and the rebels, who don't have the means to defeat them. Should we help or not? Hesitation. Procrastination. The risks involved are very real and, indeed, it is impossible to know for sure what these revolutions will engender. But fear of the future and of the mistakes from the past—and in particular, that disastrous colonial endeavor by George W. Bush in Iraq—cannot serve as a pretext for indecision and inaction. Just as it was impossible to support the Gulf War in 2003, it is impossible not to attempt to assist the Libyan rebels.

The worst, perhaps, is how conscious we are that such procrastination can, in the end, contribute to the failure of this Arab Spring awakening, of this wonderful movement, which began in Tunisia and Egypt, and is currently seeking to acquire balance and legitimacy. Politics is also the art of welcoming the unknown—that shapeless mass of "what is happening"—the power of what is to come, the way Hannah Arendt meant it.

Yet, the fear of unbalance still prevails very often. Faced with new situations, most politicians tend to want to reduce those unknowns to "known." Instead of embracing complexity and determining action that would take such complexity into consideration, they play it by ear, based on the contradictory winds of a moving and tumultuous situation, and, most importantly, based on the waves of public opinion they cunningly measure through quantitative and qualitative polls. I have the unpleasant feeling that politics is increasingly aimed at pleasing leaders of opinion, journalists, and commentators, rather than the people.

The Westphalian Trap

As concerns the Arab revolutions, I am well aware of the difficulty of the situation. Syria came later and proves my point. It is, in fact, one of the most complicated situations in which diplomacy may find itself...and of course, the point is not to declare who holds the solution. Rather, this is a perfect case in which the words of someone like Dany are welcome. Channeling him, I'd like to say that if we don't act fast, we're going to contribute to the ruin of something potentially paramount for the Mediterranean—and for all of us. If we wait until later, we will have to find different means than the ones presently at our disposal and hit harder. Only here's the thing: Assad is supreme ruler at home. So are we allowed to intervene?

Ah, that beautiful concept of 'sovereignty!' We are caught in this paradoxical world in which most fluctuations seem to overlook borders, but which remain nonetheless dominated by the illusion of borders. In 1648, *Cujus regio, ejus religio*[85] represents a crucial moment in our political evolution. By calling everyone home, the Peace of Westphalia represents the moment in our here and now in which Europe unlearns political universality, deeming

---

[85]   This Latin expression, which most readily translates to "whose religion, whose reign," was a law which stipulated that whomever was in power (the ruler) obtained the right to impose his religion upon his lands.

that a king represents a better option than a pope, all in the name of religious freedom. It originates from a rather positive belief.

After building national communities under the protection of those great Westphalian principles for three centuries, and in the light of the terrible excesses caused by nation-centered reasoning, it is time now to begin a new chapter in the history of contemporary politics.

As Cohn-Bendit pointed out about forty years ago, we spoke of containing dictatorships through democracy. We resigned ourselves to the rule of certain dictatorships, while searching for ways in which to bypass them, and consequently contributed to a change in rule. Today, it's the opposite. A portion of the American administration, or Iran or Israel for diverging reasons, seek to contain democracy through dictatorships.

That wave, which originated in Tunisia and propagated from Egypt to Libya, puts Bahrain and Saudi Arabia at risk. From the American point of view, Saudi Arabia at risk means the barrel is at two hundred dollars, which is completely unacceptable. Saudi Arabia is an indispensable pawn in the chess game that is being played by Americans in the Middle East for the sake of oil. This, of course, explains the initial hesitations of the Americans in regards to Gaddafi and their hope to contain the movement. The Israelis, meanwhile, don't know a thing, and don't want to know either, so convinced do they remain by the idea that Saudi Arabia remains their closest ally in this whole situation. And Iran lives in fear that this fire will eventually reach its borders .

Saudi Arabia, for its part, exhibited the same blind, conservative dedication to supporting Gaddafi—at least in the beginning—when, in fact, faced with this wave, true courage should have called for the opposite reaction in the form of support, reform, and liberalization. But for change to come about, oil would need to find its way out of our strategic thinking, and it is too soon to say. In 1848, the European governments didn't take into consideration the spring of the people with such enthusiasm and courage toward the reforms.

War and peace: nations against the law

The bonds between war and peace are hard to break—it's a bit like health and disease; they are two states that are defined by one another. But their connection is ontological in that it is nearly hard to even conceive of the state of perpetual peace toward which we all aspire. The experience of war influences the experience of peace. Because of this, to a certain extent, warriors are the best peace-makers, because they know its cost. After all, it's through the taking up of arms that I discovered the diplomacy of peace. But I am not a pacifist in the literal sense of the term. If I often happen to paraphrase Gandhi and his "sometimes pacifism is not enough," it is because I think a distinction must be made between pacifism and non-violence.

I know pacifism. I've practiced pacifism. In the 1920s–1930s, I was very pacific—at a time, as a matter of fact, when it might have been better to be a little less so. But we lived that era in the heavy shadow of the abominable disaster that had been the Great War. For nearly everyone, the memory of 14-18 was intolerable and we had to ensure it wouldn't repeat itself. In my eyes, as in the eyes of many of my contemporaries, Maginot was a man who was remarkable in all aspects.

In 1938, when Daladier returned from Munich, I genuinely believed he and Chamberlain had been right to do everything they could to avoid a new conflict. As a matter of fact, I remember a conversation with my love of the time, to whom I said enthusiastically, "Ah! That's it. We have peace!" She looked at me and uttered, "Do you really believe it?" I wanted to believe it, but she was the one who was right when she abruptly cut in, "You're wrong. We fucked up." I have to say that she was more mature and had more life experience.

Today, I certainly wouldn't call myself a pacifist, or with that attitude, say that all war must be avoided. I feel, rather, in full agreement with the founders of the United Nations, who planned for an international militia, which can intervene in conflicts. I am even very disappointed and bitter that this militia does not exist yet more fully. The Blue Berets are not even a start. They are soldiers who impose themselves between two countries that have already made the decision not to fight each other anymore and are merely there to ensure they don't go back at it. But there has never been, save a few exceptions—perhaps for a few years in the Congo and at one time in Cambodia—true intervention in terms of fighting a country.

Most importantly, the most outstanding failure of the Blue Berets is Bosnia, where they were never allowed to intervene militarily. From that same time period we could also mention Rwanda; but the war there had already taken a different shape.

This brings us back to the trap presented by the sovereignty of governments. It's time now to proclaim that the sovereignty of governments can no longer take precedence over the observance of human rights. When a sovereign government openly holds human rights in contempt; I deem that the United Nations should be in their full right to fight against that country, rather than being limited to mere sanctions and recommendations.

Some will object, with reason, that it is a little utopian, or naïve, to hope that the Security Council—or, in other words, that governments, political representatives—might be capable of making the judgment call that a crime is being committed here or there against human rights, and that the people must be defended against their oppressors. In fact, it is very difficult to place such faith in an organism whose members remain submitted, to such an extent, to contradictory geopolitical and national interests. But it is what I call the "evolution of law." And nowhere else than in Europe has the preeminence of law over the sovereignty of governments really progressed.

Europe has quite a fantastic characteristic: our states trust the law. It's quite rare in the world. Europeans believe in the law and believe that it is possible for it to apply to all. It is this particularly high consideration for the law that gave us the ability to create the International Criminal Court. I cannot help but find it both exciting and remarkable that it is possible to tell this or that tyrant, this or that butcher at The Hague that his actions are outlawed, based on universal texts, that his crimes (of war, against humanity, genocidal) make him subject to international judgment. It is a powerful notion, though still in its infancy.

On its end, the Security Council has managed, in certain rare moments, to rise, in the name of the law, in opposition to a sovereign state. The invasion of Kuwait by Saddam Hussein, in 1990, was the best example of this, even if this first Gulf War and its consequences were far from constituting any model of international justice.

The question of intervention in Libya presented itself exactly in those terms. In the face of the unbearable, of crimes such as the ones that Gaddafi had committed, intervention imposed itself. Only in this case, to intervene against a tyrant of a sovereign state, we needed the consent of many sovereign states—and in particular China and Russia, two rather diffident countries that feared those unfortunate precedents and other worries intervening could conceivably cause them.

Russia and China—two permanent members of the Security Council with a right to veto. The irony: this institution of the United Nations that fancies itself guarantor of international law, where I have worked so extensively, where I have lived for many hours, and to whose development I attempted to contribute, appears too often as the place *par excellence* where we encounter all obstructions to the rights of human beings. That is why it must be reformed, and in depth at that, by finally taking into account the new distribution of powers in the world: India, Japan, Brazil, and other countries that prove to us every day that the structure of the Security Council is obsolete.

Unfortunately, the Charter of the United Nations was founded on the very idea that there should be a unique place where we can decide on war and peace, and that it would be the Security Council. As for the right of veto, what happened was simple: it was the only way for Roosevelt to convince his allies, in particular Stalin, to accept this new world organization in defense of the peace he was looking to establish and take part in. Stalin would never have accepted without the assurance of being able to block decisions too opposed to his own interests. As a matter of fact, the Korean war of 1950–1953, which began against his will with a mandate of the UN (in his absence, while he was temporarily refusing to rule), reminded him of it. The notion of veto is therefore rooted in protecting the interests of two superpowers. It was one of the gridlocks of the cold war and of bipolarization.

Those five superpowers needed the assurance that they would not become a minority. And all those who, like my friend Brian Urquhart, have attempted to reform the Security Council, both expanded and with the required majority, have come up against the Five who refuse to envisage the end of their supremacy. It's a Catch-22. "Is there a single example in the history of man where someone has voluntarily abandoned the absolute control he or she beheld?" We must find way of breaking this vicious cycle.

In hoc signo vinces:
expanding the limits of our national dreams

The legend of Constantine the Great, the first Christian Roman Emperor, tells that, in 312, on the eve of a decisive battle, he saw in a dream—the standard divinatory medium in the cultures of Antiquity—a vision of the cross as symbol of his election and emblematic of his victory. This sign is his imperial dream, his dream of absolute power, the union of the altar and of the throne renewed in a more modern form for those times. It's the dream of the conquerors, those who know no limits in their appetite for adventures and grandeur.

Our nations still depend on this type of dream and power. The only regulator of such fantasies, however, is democracy—and still, that is not always the case because imperial or imperialist forms of democracy do exist, as in, for instance, the USA or Israel. A good example of democracy at work in its regulating role is perhaps the confrontation between the non-violent Ghandi and a British democracy.

If Ghandi managed to free India, it is, after all, because England was a democracy and the images of a pacific movement so violently suppressed were unacceptable to the public. Even if you must sometimes struggle to establish it, I believe non-violence to be an efficient form action within democracy or to the democratic aspirations of societies.

Let's come back to the topic of Israel and the Middle East for a moment. In a certain way, Israel is behaving toward Palestinians as many other nations have toward others in their history—like France in Algeria, for instance. So why isn't international law prevailing as an underlying guide to our reaction? The Goldstone Report of 2009 should have served as grounds for a reaction on behalf the Security Council, perhaps even grounds for a revolution, even if this had meant placing certain pressures, or even sanctions, against the nation of Israel, which has now gone way over the line. But no. The pressure was applied instead to the Goldstone Report. There should be some way in which to oppose ourselves to a certain behavior, to a certain sovereign nation, which happens to be a member of the United Nations when it breaks certain fundamental rules.

Law is at the heart of this Israeli-Palestinian issue. The situation will remain indissoluble as long as the conflict, which results from an absolutistic interpretation of history, remains unequal in force and legitimacy. There are a few of us, however, who happen to believe that Israel should be forced to stop dwelling within this particular perspective of history and come back to reality. Cohn-Bendit suggested a few times, for instance, that the United Nations General Assembly should, through a solemn vote, officially and immediately recognize the Palestinian states that exist within the borders drawn up in 1967. Perhaps it will be done.

It is true that, even if it were to be recognized, the nation of Palestine would not yet have true authority over its own territory; but in my opinion it would be an important step in rectifying those breaches in international law and finally setting the record straight. In addition, and this is where the idea becomes subtle, recognizing the Palestinian nation in its 1967 borders would, at the same time, enable us to immediately recognize the legitimacy of an Israeli state within the same borders. It's a way to force the legitimacy of the Hebrew state—upon even the most idealistic Palestinians—within borders that invalidate the persistent fantasy of the unconditional return of all refugees. Both sides will win, and both will lose.

Such is a realist's conception of the law, which seeks to balance wants and desires, which dismantles our hopes of holding absolute power, born from the feeling that our point of view, over anyone else's, is morally justified. It is a European view indeed, but a universalistic view too that we recognize first in the spirit of Roman law, as put forth by Caracalla, all through its more recent developments with the likes of Hans Kelsen and René Cassin.

Why law? Because law is the only limit to our desires. Cohn-Bendit, who knows something about desire, explains that the actual success of the dreams in nation-building that underpin the whole Israeli-Palestinian conflict depends upon each side's respective ability to curb that dream. As he says, "The Zionist dream can only exist within the confines of its limits." This suggests a return to the secular and socialist roots of Zionism, which have become a little too stifled today by a more theological interpretation. The same goes for the Palestinians, who actually experience a similar problem illustrated by an internal conflict between opposing political and theological visions of their nation's dream.

Populations and nations must, to coexist, be able to auto-limit their dreams. And what is international law if not an elucidation of what each is in his or her right to demand?

The theological or moral justifications behind the dreams of nations are always fodder for war. *Jehovah*, *Allah*, *Shoah*, *Nakba*, etc.: all of those concepts are as many moral justifications toward an absolutist legal system, meaning a system that rejects anything that seeks to limit it. These are concepts that inherently rule out politics and keep it out of matters where it would, unfortunately, be quite useful: conflict resolution.

In matters of international law, the Israeli example, among others, is dear to me because the nation of Israel was created by a resolution of the United Nations and of the Security Council. At the outcome of the war there was, of course, a consensus estimating that it was legitimate for the Jews to possess a nation. In 1948, the most powerful member nations of the time made the decision to impose this created country to a people who were not yet the Palestinians, but at the time the Arabs of Transjordan.

I remember well the negotiations, at the time, over the conditions the British would require to leave Palestine. With their Haganah, among other things, the Jews had done what they needed for the British to throw in the towel and agree to pull out. Yet, the British had a rather good understanding of the whole region and a real Arab agenda. Lawrence was still very fresh in everyone's minds. And they did decide to split the territory.

How did they go about it? Those who took part in it, like that poor Count Bernadotte or my friend back then, Ralph Bunche, negotiated blueprints believing Israel needed a nation that would be sufficiently easy to defend against surrounding Arab nations, which would be accomplished by providing the Jews with 55 percent of the territory and the Arabs with 45 percent. The Israelis accepted the resulting compromise for nearly twenty years. The problem is that one of the two parties quickly became very powerful. Militarily, Israel could quite easily defeat the Arab states that contested the international decision, and it succeeded in expanding its borders—moving from 55 percent to 78 percent into Palestine.

Until 1967, the Israelis lived in a portion of Palestine that was consistent with the sectioning sanctioned by international law. Jehovah no longer ruled. The Security Council did. The Israelis accepted the conditions and might have accepted them for longer yet if they hadn't had the miserable luck of winning the Six-Day War in such extraordinary circumstances, which went to their heads, like a sort of *hybris* that justifies everything, including this desire to conquer the whole region, as it is the promised land "granted by God."

They therefore placed God up against international law. Who can win in such conditions? God is strong, especially when backed by people who believe in him. And, as a matter of fact, even when backed by people who do not believe in him—for there are many secular citizens in Israel who simply accept the *fait accompli*.[86] International law reacted immediately, and, oddly, with a unanimous agreement of the Security Council, and two resolutions were successively adopted: number 242 and 338. Those resolutions

---

[86]   Translates literally to "the done deed"

clearly stated that the occupation was not legitimate, that the borders of 1967 had to be reinstated, that Jerusalem had to be the capital of two nations, and that there needed to be a territory for all of the refugees.

This stance, adopted by entities responsible for upholding the law, by the Security Council, by the General Assembly, and by the International Court of Justice, was completely ignored, even held in contempt by Israel, which did nothing toward complying with international law, and instead, every time negotiations began, worked toward their failure. They were collaborating only on the face of it. Palestine, a land of people with a right to a nation, has only existed, finally, since the start of this whole Israeli-Palestinian conflict. But little by little, with important and intelligent people like Arafat, it has become an almost-nation, or at the very least, a respected power that the Israelis nevertheless succeed in dividing quite easily in testing times that often proved to be inconsequential.

The key, in this conflict, is really this idea of "auto-limitation." And it isn't a concept that should only apply in the case of the Middle East; we must find it at the heart of the European adventure too. It's the opposite of the *hybris*. The law wants us to accept limitations upon our dreams. For a long time, France held its own fantasies in regards to its natural borders and its colonies; Britain too had its empire; Germany, its Third Reich; and today, Washington fancies itself an Athens of the twenty-first century. Auto-limitation ends the dream that might challenge the law. It regulates desire, thanks to the law. The law grows, little by little. The law forces modesty upon those who pine for control.

If men were perfect, they wouldn't need an outside law; but in the absence of auto-regulation by the conscience, we need the law, which looks to control us. Let us add intelligence to the mix. I think that we find the intelligence of a given population in its ability to recognize the limitation of its dreams as prescribed by the law. We do not experience the law emotionally. We experience the dream emotionally, and that which the emotion confronts itself to is the law. Someone might think, "I am elected. I would like to... But I cannot. There is the law." Our intelligence should cause us to curb our emotions.

It's a practice of asceticism and of self-improvement transposed to the field of politics.

Human Applause[87]

Has love not hallowed, filled with new life my heart,
With lovelier life? Then why did you prize me more
When I was proud and wild and frantic
Lavish of words, yet in substance empty?

The crowd likes best what sells in the marketplace,
And loud-mouthed force alone wins a slave's respect.
In gods and godhead only he can
Truly believe who himself is godlike.

---

[87] Hölderlin, Friedrich. *Selected Poems and Fragments*. Trans. Michael Hamburger. Ed. Jeremy D. Adler. London: Penguin, 1998. 11. Print.

Eight

Democracy: What A Plan!

Ending oligarchy

With the wisdom of my ninety-four years, I can now tell you what my long life has taught me: we can succeed in our efforts. We have watched the collapse of fascism, Stalinism, apartheid, and the colonization of innumerable peoples. We have watched democracy triumph. But what are the implications of democracy?

Let's first begin by reminding ourselves of what Churchill once said: democracy is the worst form of government except for all those others; and now, let us hark back to Aristotle whose other forms of government included tyranny (the rule of one supported by the people's 'voluntary servitude'), oligarchy (rule of the few – perhaps the 'best' few, but who quickly earn a privileged status), and democracy (rule by and for the people). Some of those terms lack necessary clarity. What is meant by, "*the people*?" What does it mean "*to rule*?" And finally, what makes a leader a mentor in the eyes of his or her people rather than a "*ruler*?" Such leaders do exist. Let us not doubt it.

The Christians say, "God exists. I have met him." I have not met God; but I have met Pierre Mendès France, Mikhail Gorbachev, Nelson Mandela, and also the Dalai Lama and Aung San Suu Kyi. Above all, however, I was fortunate enough to work alongside Franklin Delano Roosevelt on the Charter of the United Nations, a document into which he poured his heart and soul, and which he based off of the four freedoms delineated in the Atlantic Charter—a founding text for one of the most ambitious institutions of the past few centuries and which also happens to hold an account of the fundamental values underlying democracy.

The Charter begins with the words "We the peoples" and, for the first time in our recent centuries, moves the rights of human beings to center stage. The respect and promotion of those values was and still must be integral to all Member Nations (today we count one-hundred-and-ninety-three) of the new organization for each to be considered, in the fullest sense of the term, true democracies.

But again, what kind of democracy are we referring to? The trap Westerners have fallen into, by insisting upon categorically rejecting the idea of 'people's democracies,' such as the ones that took shape in the East, has been to link democracy with political and economic liberalism.

We must, of course, protect, preserve and make our freedoms known; namely the four pulled from the Atlantic Charter, upon which Roosevelt and Churchill finally came to an agreement in the middle of the ocean after their long ideological butting of heads: Freedom of expression, freedom of confession, freedom from fear, freedom from want. But it is this last one in particular that makes true democracy incompatible with a free, deregulated market.

What we should also note is that, in June of 1945, in San Francisco, where the Charter that begins with "We the people" (and which will come to define democracy as the ruling form of government) was adopted; those four freedoms were called back and into the Preamble by those who were drafting it. Today, the heirs of those great principles need their own version of a 'San Francisco moment' (for indeed, they have already understood the direction in which to steer this ever-losing fight—this fight, which must be constantly revisited if we are to help the most destitute rise out of poverty so that they too may become a *demos* conscious as much of its rights as of its obligations). In fewer words, a true liberal democrat should focus his or her efforts on eradicating poverty.

The fundamental difference between oligarchy and democracy isn't just a ruling 'few' versus a 'many,' but really a '*privileged* few' versus an '*underprivileged* many.' To take action so that the underprivileged may become a class of thriving people: such should be a democracy's main aim, but sadly is no longer. With this in mind, all criticism of people's democracies is perfectly legitimate, and is precisely the reason why the very concept of 'democracy' needs to be promoted as an agenda in and of itself.

When they are legitimate, texts aren't ever just mere statements of fact; they are a plan. The Universal Declaration of Human Rights, for instance, is a plan. The devoted democrat has but one plan: to provide all people with access to what they are entitled to, in the name of their equality in both freedoms and rights; or, in other words, the devoted democrat seeks to invest in an effort that directly aims to help the underprivileged rise out of their underprivileged class. In a certain way, this gets us back into Walter Benjamin, for what Benjamin describes as the true subject of historical cognition is the battling of the oppressed class itself, slaves and others, and the lasting nature of their grievances.

This questioning of democracy and of the nature of the democratic government toward which we are steering ourselves is primordial. We must constantly ask ourselves: What is democracy exactly? True democrats are leaders who emphasize, above all, the importance of helping the greatest number of individuals attain the highest level of knowledge, education, health, and shelter. Those are true democrats.

In an interview, Peter Sloterdijk alleged that the problem of democracy is that people do not want to be equals; they want to be favorites. "Being equal but irrelevant interests no one. The perfect democracy would be one in which we would have mastered the art of favoring everyone." It's an amusing view, and only absurd upon initial reflection. For indeed, this desire to be favored should not be afforded only to a select few, but really a door left open for all to enter.

As for oligarchy, what is it exactly? It is that privileges are inherent for a select few: those who are in power and have responsibilities. For them to have privileges is all good and well. They should have privileges (not too many, of course) for the government to remain stable. But starting with Aristotle, it is only when the entirety of a population ascends, through its education, to a certain level of empowerment, and thereby has increased the level of responsibility it can assume, that the plan for democracy truly moves into action.

Democracy and ecology

Let's return to this notion of a plan for a moment. Democracy is never a given. Never. It is a tangible utopia we must achieve. There are some individuals who have, with a similar ambition as mine, worked toward providing everyone with everything, and who then became totalitarians. We need Hannah Arendt to analyze at each instant how such a thing can occur, and how we are tricked into it.

The other trap that is particularly difficult to avoid today is that of conservative Neoliberalism, of the "Washington consensus," for instance, inspired by economists like Milton Friedman. Let's just let the market, and nothing but the market, do its thing with no further government interference in the growth of the economy. If the best, the most audacious, the most capable of making a profit, and of accumulating resources are left free—"go get rich," as François Guizot used to say—everything will be fine. Well, no. Everything will go horribly, as the recent crises have undeniably proven.

A different kind of plan deserves our engagement today. We must charge the political powers that be with a mission, a mandate allowing them to impose certain rules upon the market, which will force it to serve the people.

The market's role should situate itself halfway between the role it would occupy in a communist ideology, which has now become totalitarianism, and the role it would have in an economic liberal ideology, which has now become this giant, tentacular being. The market should operate in that precious and fragile space, which finds itself, time and time again, threatened by our two libidos: our *libido dominandi* and our *libido possidendi*, or tyranny and greed. Preserving this space has become yet more important now that we have discovered how severely industrial corporations are encroaching upon the natural equilibriums that are supposed to help ensure the continuation of our presence on this planet. And it is for that reason too that we must become engaged both in a fight for social justice *and* in a fight to preserve the environment.

In a Marxist-liberal approach, the question is never whether or not to create wealth, but rather how to proceed with redistribution. Yet, today, it is obvious that an unlimited system of production is literally unsustainable, and one needs only to read Edgar Morin to become convinced of the fact that we cannot solve the issue of social justice without solving environmental issues too. Moreover, it is precisely when a democratic plan espouses both those ideas that it becomes easier to enlist the active participation of young people, who look forward to the prospect of both defending their planet and reducing poverty. I simply wish that ecologists and socialists, each on their own sides, would fully grasp the interdependence of both those issues in helping true democracy actualize itself.

Militants for legal rights are militants for an ideal

My faith in the value of international law and the role of the United Nations in our increasingly fragmented, nationalitarian, and balkanized contemporary world (and, as a result, a world wary of embryos of worldwide governance such as the UN) may have surprised that of others, but this faith is rooted in my experience of history. It seems to me that someone who has experienced World War II, and who experienced, in particular, its most painful parts, cannot rid him-or herself of the immeasurable hope represented by that extraordinary, revolutionary document, The Charter of the United Nations. The thinking of its creator, President Roosevelt, was based on a similar experience of history. It was out of the question for him that the values of honor with which we defeated National Socialism and fascism should fail to be encapsulated in this universal document of reference for all human societies.

The Charter's context was innovative. The first innovation was to open this organization to all peoples, and not only to all nations. The second was to make it an organization aimed at preventing war; but also making the rights of human beings the fundamental value upon which the new world was to be built. Utopic? Naïve? I believe, on the contrary, that the institution itself and the documents it has produced capture, embody, and carry with them the proof of the progress made by our human societies. It is a slow and painful progress, but one that has occurred, as both those documents and the institution itself continue, decade after decade, to promote democracy throughout the world and provide all peoples with the option of recourse to international law.

As to my numerous friends who impart their skepticism of realists upon me (and with good reason), I would like to invite them all to be truly realist and observe the following facts: have we not already accomplished great things, made significant strides? Through those very imperfect institutions, those international organizations for civil aviation, telecommunications, health, work, education, science, and culture, we have already achieved much more important things than we ever could have imagined: we have set the foundations for a global society and for worldwide regulations.

Régis Debray presented me with an amusing and very pertinent revisiting of self-limitation (the concept I was touching upon earlier) within the bounds of Freudian principles. He suggested considering the UN as a sort of superego. In each national community, the id, the subconscious, or the *libido dominandi* and its aggressive impulses would prevail. The self, working itself into all affairs of the nation, this global superego would then be left to act as a sort of meddler—let's label it a censoring agent, called upon here and there to rectify this or that vile impulse of the world's magma. The metaphor is delightful—it makes of human rights the regulating ideal and the UN a type of conscience of the collective un-conscious. I really like this way of positing the issue: the UN seen as an organ of civilizing repression, taming our ancient savage core, and the image of the superego fits perfectly. I might add too that, in that space between the subconscious and the global superego, there is the wide spectrum of how we actually conduct ourselves.

It is very difficult, when acting, to not be influenced by that global superego, by that bad collective conscience em-bodied by the UN. Even that bandit George W. Bush sought, until the very last moment before pouncing into Baghdad, to gain legitimacy through the Security Council's approval. Therefore, even when they are not respected, those texts tend to influence our actions—merely through their ex-istence. Unlike "the realists" would like to believe, it isn't only national sovereignty and financial stability that make them relevant. Reality itself is subject to the influence of the superego.

A long life has also provided me with a high degree of de-tachment. In ninety-four years, I've had time to watch the world change, not only in appearance, but in spirit too. The wars obviously modified power relations in the world, but the Charter of the United Nations and the Universal Declaration of Human Rights have helped to shape that power. I am con-vinced that certain contemporary solutions to very old prob-lems, such as international regulation, would have seemed completely wild around the time of my birth, and perhaps even some twenty or forty years later. But today, those solu-tions have been implemented. For instance, human rights isn't just a concept—they are the European Court of Human Rights, which can prosecute European nations and make them accountable for their actions. They are that embryonic International Criminal Court too that can now prosecute the Pinochets, the *Miloševic*s, and the Charles Taylors of the world.

Now, you must not accuse me of being naïve. I know full well that some of the world's great powers neither subscribe to such Courts nor have they ratified them. The Americans, for instance, cannot consent to having one of their citizens judged by a foreigner. Israel and China have a similarly possessive interpretation of the prerogatives of the sovereign authority of their State. Régis Debray actually draws attention to the problem: The risk here is to end up with this Nietzschean reading of the law, in which the weakest end up complying with some regulations that remain disputed by the strong, who, for their part, believe they need to answer to no one.

This attitude is precisely what contributed to the success of that neoconservative essayist Robert Kagan on the topic of Europe, around the time of the Iraq war: let the Europeans churn in their mirage of Kantian peace; they are post-historical.

We have so far mentioned Freud and Nietzsche. Only the third crony of the great skeptics is missing at roll call— and indeed, there is another criticism aimed at the philosophy of human rights of which Régis Debray, among others, reminded me recently and that we must consider.

In his article, "The Jewish Question" (1844), Marx explains that human rights are the rights of an individual once he has been literally stripped of his human parts. In other words, they are the rights of the bourgeoisie to be selfish, to act according to its individual interests; they are man separated from his community, his past, his class, his country. According to Marx, human rights reflect an ideology of world gentrification, the triumph of the individual and of his short-term interests over his natural and social environment.

Marx's skepticism is strong and his criticism is valid: do human rights risk, at a certain point, becoming a weapon in the proliferation of individualism in this world? Are they to simply become an ideological weapon in the hands of the strongest, who own the market and whose ideas are, therefore, dominant?

It is hard for me to watch human rights invoked in the way they are sometimes: in the name of superior civilizations one day; in the name of a certain concept of gender equality or to protect minorities the next; and then also sometimes to make a case against certain parts of the world (where such rights are not respected) and condemn them as extra-historical or backwards societies onto whom it is acceptable to impose, by force or by armed colonization, the respect of those universal values. This paradox, this obvious contradiction, this "double standard" as the Anglo-Saxons call it, is to be expected—but it is terrible. We must draw a line somewhere. Marx's criticism is only partially correct. It addresses the historical experience of bourgeois domination and its imperialist discourse; but it does not invalidate the concept of human rights in itself and its ability to take on other groundbreaking forms.

At their core, the rights of a human person only have meaning if man is considered in all of his social aspects: as a part of a state-controlled, democratic community. That word again: democracy. We are back to where we started with that difficult term, and more difficult as it is adapted to fit any case.

Let us linger for just a minute more on the texts in the Universal Declaration. From the Preamble, it is clearly indicated that civil, political, economic, social, and cultural rights must be protected by a democratic rule, in absence of which, man will once again be brought to revolt against tyranny or oppression. This is a true sign that those texts were not written "post-historically," and that we were not at the time ignorant about relations between nations, or of the dangers of the desire for power and the desire for domination, as denounced by Marx in his notion of the Bourgeois-citizen and the sham that is a liberal democratic rule. I am perfectly aware that the Declaration of Human Rights and all it involves is part of a plan that is still far from being complete. Will it ever be?

Of Mutability[88]

Still, still upon my cheek I feel their breath:
How can it be that days which seem so near
Are gone, forever gone, and lost in death?

This is a thing that none may rightly grasp,
A thing too dreadful for the trivial tear:
That all things glide away from out our clasp;

And that this I, unchecked by years, has come
Across into me from a little child.
Like an uncanny creature, strangely dumb;—

That I existed centuries past—somewhere,
That ancestors on whom the earth is piled
Are yet as close to me as my very hair.

As much a part of me as my very hair.

[88]   Hofmannsthal, Hugo Von. *The Lyrical Poems: Hugo Von Hofmannsthal. Transl. from the German with an Introd. by Charles Wharton Stork.* Trans. Charles W. Stork. New Haven [u.a.: Yale Univ., 1918. Print.

Nine

"The Immobile Scatters and the Moving Remains"[89]

Demanding the ideal

I may seem like one of those dreamers who are miles off from the actual world, but I want to keep hoping that a deep change in the functioning of human societies is possible. What might seem illusory today doesn't make it less of a believable and reachable goal.

True realism calls for us to take note of human potential, rather than of its limitations in the face of resignation. That

---

[89] Hessel's original quote is "L'immobile se disperse et le mouvant demeure" which he claims is pulled from an "Hymne Shivaïque" of the sixth century (a hymn to Shiva)

is the true sense of the message I am working to share with present generations and those yet to come. Our planet has not said the last of it; our brains haven't revealed themselves fully. The roads of evolution still stretch long ahead of us, and to reuse an image from my friend Edgar Morin, "A metamorphosis is possible. Out of the caterpillar the butterfly may one day arise." Does that mean we must resign ourselves to being caterpillars and having blind faith in the fact that our butterfly state will come? Or are we better off working toward helping the little caterpillar find its path toward evolution?

What may one day seem like a utopia or illusory, a lost cause, may, very plainly and simply, become a reality. For a long time, the feminists came up against the rule of tradition, against notions imposed by society, a phallocratic society at that, and limited knowledge of biology. Let's measure the ground that has been covered, our substantial progresses, and the ground yet to cover.

The Natural State, The Nature of States: globalization and freedoms

Unfortunately, the Enlightenment has somewhat waned. Yet the idea that different forms of progress, of knowledge, of techniques, of the mind, the idea that political and social progresses are all intimately linked, was a wonderful one. *What is Enlightenment?*, by Immanuel Kant, remains one of the most beautiful texts in existence, and one of the most meaningful on the collective progress of humanity. I can understand the reservations of some critics who, like Régis

Debray, believe that there are certain unavoidable patterns in human interaction, patterns which remain relatively invariant, and that human groups are, in their interactions, limited to a natural state that cannot be moved beyond, a state which imbues borders with all of their political and heuristic worth.

Yet, those very same thinkers admit that we may find progress within community. For instance, the establishment of law and democracy within the framework of a nation-state is an improvement within a given community. But as soon as we look to move beyond national borders and onto talks of globalism, those thinkers shrink back into that same old idealist/realist divide.

Therefore, improvement is only ever possible within a defined national community. So that there may be human rights, there must be a constitutional state. It's the state that enforces the law. But such an approach makes the state the key to everything, and today we can only worry about the shapes globalization is taking—most of which tend to exclude the state. Should the producer of norms (the government) and the keeper of their peace (the police, justice) be made to disappear? What would happen to the rights of a person?

Must we therefore defend the sovereignty of nations in the name of human rights? This is only a paradox on the surface. So long as I can remember, Hegel is the philosopher who most impacted me in my youth. As I understood Hegelian philosophy, it illustrated a current of history moving toward increasing freedoms: slaves prevailing over their masters, imposing freedom, until a democratic state resulted. In short, a state of law marked the outcome of an odyssey toward freedom, since individual rights were finally respected. Considering these matters on an international scope upsets this balance. For each nation is merely an island among others, master of its own domain, and indifferent to what happens elsewhere. Our Westphalian heritage: nations are responsible for enforcing their own laws.

What is left of the universality of those rights? The stakes here are that universalism should triumph over the savage and hawkish competition between nations. The wars and spectacular destruction caused over the course of the twentieth century ask that we consider the implementation of global regulations. For rights to be universally respected, must we change the scope of our thinking and build a world state?

Let's be realistic. The model of the nation-state (cultural unity, democratic interplay) is not suitable, or at least no longer suitable. I am of those who have for a long time considered that we should put into place the elements necessary for a true world government—entering into a co-existence of nations, which would each retain their prerogatives and democratic responsibilities, but which would be enjoined to learn to work together in such a way that those fundamental values would be respected everywhere. Hard? Surely. Impossible? Certainly not. There is no reason for the international stage to remain Hobbes's realm when nations have adopted Hegel.

As a matter of fact, in the example of the Israeli-Palestinian issue I touched upon earlier, we have on the one side a right that is unable to confirm itself as an obligation, on the other forces that cannot be disproved. Between this military, economic, and political supremacy that is unable to produce an equitable situation, and the rights of the Palestinians supported by some perfectly abstract notions of international law that everyone scorns—to which a mere allusion is taken as a quasi anti-Semitic provocation—we've reached a gridlock.

There are countries that feel confident enough to emancipate themselves from the rules imposed by the community. We always speak of the United States and Israel, but we should also mention Morocco, which, in the case of Eastern Sahara, remains as obstinate and unjust as Israel is toward the Palestinians. What both these failures have in common is the "international community," which is responsible for ensuring that the law is respected. Unfortunately, the nations that constitute this international community are more concerned with defending their own interests than with enforcing and upholding the law, of which they are nevertheless the guarantors, since they are signatories of those founding documents.

As for the idea that law without enforcement is futile, I do not automatically draw the conclusion that force alone matters. Instead, I conclude that we have not yet put into place the means to limit the sovereignty of nations when they overstep their rights, or when they fail at their responsibilities and cease to provide a framework which guarantees the exercise of fundamental rights. One of those means is the conscience of the citizens. During the war of Algeria, this rise in awareness—gradual, belated, tactless, yet true—was what finally resulted in the demand for a cease-fire and earned support for General de Gaulle's impulse toward decolonization.

Unfortunately, those influences are missing in Israel and in Morocco. Could they perhaps be mobilized outside of those borders? Such is the motivation behind my engagement to promote a Russell Tribunal on Palestine. Of course, such action is highly symbolic: the tribunal neither has a police force, nor an administration to help carry out its sentence. But it's an initiative that looks to cultivate consciences and help the great problems, which seem insolvable, become, little by little, solvable. Thanks to the actions of a convinced few—as, today, the members of the Russell Tribunal on Palestine, and, in the past, on Vietnam—thanks to people taking a stand, to texts that remind us of unbearable and inadmissible abuses, certain causes are able to be advanced.

I insist upon the idea that idealism tends to exert a certain influence upon our actions and transforms us, bit by bit—a process by which we essentially become different from what we are by nature. By nature, we of course remain bound to our wish for self-preservation, to those impulses that cause us to mistrust what could actually improve us. But I remain convinced that the impetus of an ideal can move into action even the most indolent minds.

Transcendences of the worlds: a certain idea of the planet

Here I am, all of a sudden, starting to sound like a German philosopher, like Sloterdijk, meandering calmly down Heidelberg's *Philosophenweg*—in the same shade that once wrapped Hegel, Fichte, and the others two centuries ago—meditating over the ruses of history, the meaning of work, the mind and its inventions.

When I turn philosophical, it's in order to understand all of my experiences, to derive from them a more complete view. Camus said something along the lines of "understanding is unifying." All said and done, there must be something about my being-in-the-world and in the way I have lived that has helped to shape my soul somehow. To remain untouched by that which we take part in, what we live through and do, without growing inside or deriving any lessons—well, it's a bit of a waste.

I believe phenomenology helps us understand to what extent we are not only all connected in our perception of the truth, which is based on hard facts; but that certain "essences" exist, which allow us to analyze what occurs around us in a way that doesn't only make sense for us personally, but that is consubstantial with the events themselves. In practice, all who wish to exploit it share the fact of oil. When we are concerned with the *Wesentliches*, or the essential, we cease to be in the *Eigentumliches*, or the particular. And that is how, it seems to me, all civilizations evolve.

Let's come back to this process of civilization for a moment. It is in that long process of domestication of violence, of the establishment of a public, religious, or secular moral code, that human societies have progressively put an end to a certain number of pointless violences. The limits to this process are that it remains internal to a given community or society. There will come a time when this civilization will find itself to be singular in the multitude of different communities all capable of mutually recognizing each other as equally valid and legitimate.

But this global moral code…what can it be? Planet-wide ecology?

Jean-Claude Carrière shared with me his reasoning, that of an anthropologist, traveling writer, and Buddhist disciple, by returning to this notion of interdependence. The problem, according to him, and I don't believe that he is wrong, is that our Western way of thinking is more anxious to analyze and classify than to understand and unify. We live here, in the West, in a separate world, where we put everything in boxes, in neat little drawers.

As it turns out, it's what Edgar Morin constantly reproaches in our Western education system: its systematic propensity to compartmentalize knowledge, which prevents the interaction of ideas. Jean-Claude Carrière also evokes the famous philosophical law of the excluded middle; in other words, a thing is this or that and *tertium non datur*, there is no third way. Peter Sloterdijk has already criticized and defeated the theory of this binary logic at length in his books—in particular in *La Domestication de l'être*[90]—I therefore feel in perfect continuity here.

Let's come back to the Asian—but not just Buddhist—traditions. They happen to offer an interpretation that is diametrically opposed to this notion of compartmentalization: things are this *and* that, and in all life there is death. In the

---

[90]   Sloterdijk, Peter. *La Domestication de l'être: pour un éclaircissement de la clairière.* Paris: Éditions Mille Et Une Nuits, 2000. Print. Note: No English translation of this book is currently available. The original is in German: *Domestikation des Seins: Die Verdeutlichung der Lichtung.*

Yin there is the Yang, and vice-versa. In the costume you are wearing, there is the vegetal, the animal, and God knows what else; and nothing can be picked apart from the rest. If we start trying to divide the elements that constitute reality, we are very quickly lost.

When you speak to the Dalai Lama of that word which has never been given a true, universal definition—"ecology"—he answers, very surprised and amused, "You discovered ecology thirty years ago. It's extraordinary because we have been living in the Whole for the past twenty-five hundred years." Using the Buddhist metaphor of the wheel, he adds, "You think you are the hub of the wheel, but the wheel has no hub. The cosmos revolves around nothing. There is no axe, no center, no circumference."

And yet, it turns! Each of us is one of the spokes, and we are a special spoke, a spoke with a superior power to the others: an ability to break the natural balance, to shatter the harmonious balance that makes the world go round. We are the only spoke that can do away with the other spokes.

Listening to Jean-Claude Carrière and the Dalai Lama, it seems to me that we should raise this simple little historic fact: our rise in awareness of our ecological interdependence and of our mad ability to destroy ecosystems only occurred to us from the moment when those ecosystems were truly threatened.

In the 1970s, the level of destruction brought about by that single spoke of the wheel of the world began to make itself seen. Human beings might well have kept on, believing they were the hub, if there hadn't been a rise in awareness that we were destroying the Whole, that we were gravely damaging it.

That is how, very recently, this awareness, which seems so elemental to our Eastern or Budhhist friends, came about in the West. Ecology, as we know it, is dated back to and finds its root in a rise in awareness of interdependence between man and his natural habitat as well as his global environment. My hope is that this awareness can continue to grow nearly indefinitely, and that it can become further defined and reach a form of enlightenment. Then we would no longer need to destroy anything, since we will have it all.

Individuals and multitudes in the wheel of the world

The main obstacle that remains on the path to this eventual global awareness—which is called "universal vision" in Hinduism—is a much-needed dissolution of the ego (a small difficulty raised by Jean-Claude Carrière). It's the other concept that Buddhists are alluding to when we ask them for help: impermanence. Nothing is fixed in its duration. Nothing is guaranteed to endure. Everything is at risk, including us. Not only do we never "bathe in the same river," since it runs, but on top of it, "it's never the same bather," since we too change. Jean-Claude Carrière's thinking completes Parmenides'. I think the circle is closed.

This notion of ego is truly an obsession in the West. One needs only inspect the shelves of a bookstore to realize the number of works by psychoanalysts, psychologists, and writers, which all revolve around the ego. Yet, according to

Jean-Claude Carrière, who met the Dalai Lama many times, one feels, in his presence, this extraordinary feeling of being face to face with a very smart, very relaxed, very smiling man, whose ego is impossible to define. It is impossible to say: "That is what he is." He is as if poured into everything that surrounds him. Such a state is very difficult to reach. It requires complete renouncement of this or that possession, or to this or that attachment, as a necessary step toward happiness, wherefrom the difficulty Westerners have at grasping the idea that interdependence is complementary to the impermanence of all things.

To illustrate the concept, Carrière quotes this beautiful line from a Shaivite hymn from the fifth or sixth century: "The immobile scatters and the moving remains." Motion in and of itself is a quality. And what changes remains. All that we deem immobile, stable, or durable ends up moving in the end.

We Westerners are still quite tied to the idea of a target, of a goal. Our history is linear and our religions, when they aren't too busy waiting on the end of the world or the Second Coming of a messiah, expect some growth, which, in itself, is merely linear. We are always trying to reach a target.

But what do we end up reaching exactly? I feel that through this question the issue of engagement presents itself to us in different terms. If, in a certain way, everything is always perfect, and that impermanence renders our opinion or perspective on the issue void from the very moment we have expressed it, then why should we suddenly focus on this or that problem, such as an economic crisis, the independence of this or that country, the fate of an oppressed or tortured people—how do we perpetuate energy toward all of that?

Ernst Jünger, in his *Waldgänger*,[91] considers that individual serenity is not sustainable in a world that is suffering—we cannot open yoga studios when our brothers are being tortured on the floor below. Jean-Claude Carrière asks the same question: if we want to act, we must be very concrete, focus all of our resources, be ourselves, and develop arguments. How then can we reconcile those two directives that seem so contradictory: the indignation necessary to put a will into action and the equanimity provided by a satisfied conscience?

According to me, they are possible to reconcile. I remain very tied to the idea that we have things to do in a world that is unwell. But if we began from a state of acquired serenity, perhaps we would place our faith in action, in doing what is wanted and necessary with all of the energy needed—maintaining, meanwhile, the sense, the conviction, that we are leaving our serene state only to return to it once we have completed the required action.

Therefore, we mustn't do anything that could jeopardize that balance. This, of course, requires us to make use of non-violent action: dialog, negotiation… The actions of the Dalai Lama, at the helm of the national Tibetan resistance, are a quite good illustration of such a practice, and he is the only one who has managed—and for a very long time now—to ensure that the Tibetans would not commit any terrorist ac-

---

[91]   Hessel is likely referring back to this book: Jünger, Ernst. *Der Waldgang*. Stuttgart: Klett-Cotta, 2007. Print.

tion against the Chinese. And that was done despite temptations and activist groups that would like to manifest, in a very vain and suicidal fashion, their antagonism toward the Chinese authorities. He has always succeeded in calming them and even claims to pray for the Chinese. He says it all the time. He says that there is some good in the Chinese. He will have left a mark that we can call exemplary on the issue. For me, it was a great pleasure to meet him recently, on August 13, 2011, in Toulouse, and have the opportunity to share a few words between men of good will.

Harmony and the order of nations

Finally, having looked at Heraclitus, Parmenides, and the Dalai Lama, it is possible to recognize the extraordinary shortcomings of a politics in which nations are all set against each other. And also, naturally, the shortcomings of economic and financial superpowers, similarly set against each other. For I have noticed that, despite all appearances and all of the talks on financial globalization, there has never been a true effort made toward unifying the world's economy.

Can't you just picture the bigwigs meeting in Davos for example? Why not? Meeting to discuss their wish for shared regulations and turn the immense power they hold to good by harmoniously tuning the working of the world economy, and, consequently, avoid entering into sterile competition, working instead toward a common good for humanity? I can dream, can't I?

For too many centuries we have been dominated by destructive rivalry. And, above all, by that hypocritical mockery the global oligarchy puts on. The powerful nations and their representatives, who meet in Davos or elsewhere, already know that the differences that oppose them are indissoluble. Take, for instance, the inextricable case of the conflict in the Middle East. If we take that struggle and look at it in the light of Buddhism, or with an Eastern mindset, we might be inspired by this startling precept: "My enemy is my best guru." This means that, in my enemy, whomever he may be, as fervently as I may despise him, there is something good, something just. Of course it's hard; for we always limit ourselves to such narrow views: the enemy is the enemy—he must be destroyed or beaten into submission, and *tertium non datur*, when, in fact, we can only reach a solution in seeking what the enemy can bring us. There's a good way for diplomacy to take on a previously ignored role.

In my unconditional defense of the United Nations, I always like to justify the organization as a marvelous tool that has been, up until now, poorly used. It's as if you had a full, professional symphonic orchestra, which you know has the potential to play Beethoven's *Fifth Symphony*, but which merely produces discordant rumbles for the time being. And the musicians are constantly stopping and screaming at each other, "But you're not playing the same music as I am!" What's my point?

What a waste it is to leave such a beautiful orchestra without sheet music or direction. It could have solved, perhaps it may still solve, the issue of being poorly tuned at living on the same planet. To think up the instruments was visionary. The sheet music is the law. The music is the law applied.

One time, Jean-Claude Carrière invited me to reread the book that served as the founding for the entirety of Western politics: *The Social Contract* by Rousseau. The first sentence reads, "Man was born free and everywhere he is in chains." It's a beautiful sentence, very brilliant, but which is actually wrong according to Carrière. For man is not born free of everything. He does not choose his gender, his birthplace, his religion (in most cases), much less his family or his genes. He is born anything but free. When this phrase was adapted for the Declaration of Human Rights it became, "All human beings are born free and equal in dignity and rights." The word "rights" is an absolutely essential structuring element, because if they are free and equal in their rights, it means that, *de facto*, they are not. That's precisely what the text says. My beloved Declaration is an agenda, and not a mere statement of fact.

With a relentlessness for which I am criticized, I often find myself referring to the two terms that follow: reason and conscience. In the program we drafted in 1948, you will find from the very start a call toward human conscience, toward a type of lucidity, a sense of responsibility, toward self-limitation, and also toward love and truth. Being aware of your own reason means subjecting it to its own tribunal, as Kant suggested. Only conscience can allow reason to direct reason.

And do we need it.

Symbiosis of civilizations

The future of a global collective conscience can find its source in the notion of dignity. Dignity is something concrete above all, something anchored in the truth of human situations: not having to be insulted, humiliated, or held in contempt. And this respect for human beings, through their glory as in their deepest misery, can become global. Edgar Morin actually often speaks of the "positive effects of globalization." And if it is undeniable that there are many negative effects, continuously denied by the blissful Neoliberals, there are nevertheless a few positive effects too, whatever the opinion of the bitter sovereigntists, the vengeful nationalists, or stubborn leftists. For a start, thanks to globalization, we have become aware of our interdependence.

Morin, for example, shows the enriching interpenetration of different modes of thinking in the field of medicine. We could also mention our relationship to the environment. I've already mentioned those civilizations, which have been engulfed by modernity and who view their relationship with their natural environment as a sort of dynamic balance, which could inspire new behaviors on a global scale. The East would meet the West in a type of dialog, which has now moved beyond its shared fantasies of colonialism, resistance, and Orientalism from past centuries.

Plainly, the world is evolving, and we must encourage it to do so, so it may move toward a sort of symbiosis of civilizations, where each would bring the best of his or her cultural and historical experience to counterbalance the vices of the others and where respective virtues could be combined. The rights of men and women, democracy, and individual rights are all positive aspects of modern civilization. And in the case of those longer-established civilizations and their relationship to nature, which we have lost, the sense of solidarity, which has deteriorated within us, the sense of respect, as, for instance, for the elderly whom they do not cast off into homes—these are all qualities to ponder.

This learning process should be the opportunity to finally overcome the persistent and mutilating disjunction between mind and matter so typical of the modern Western world, which tends to separate all things when they are, in fact, connected. The following lies at the heart of the reform in Morin's thought: we should view even civilizations that we deem archaic, such as the indigenous peoples in Brazil, as contributors of precious values—not only in their conception of solidarity; but also for their knowledge of the world and nature—their knowledge of the virtues of different plants, animals. Retailers have already understood it, since they seek to monopolize this knowledge to further increase their profits; but politicians are lagging behind, remaining crystallized in their arrogant Western-centeredness.

On the other hand, it's also good to recognize the merits of our own civilization. We have, for instance, in our Western tradition (and very present in the French way of thinking) a strong tendency toward self-criticism. You can find it in Montaigne and Montesquieu, and that whole tradition that carries on until Levi-Strauss. This ability toward self-criticism is also a treasure we must look to keep and disseminate, at home and beyond.

This idea of symbiosis of civilizations seems to stand in direct opposition with today's leading debates on the dangers of multiculturalism in Europe: Germany's *Leitkultur*; France's national identity debate; Finland, Denmark, and Sweden's populist, nationalist parties; Belgium, Italy, and Austria's, and even the United States' separatist regionalisms. It seems we are witness to a generalized offensive against the mix of cultures. It's understandable, in a way, that the movement of globalization and of increased interactions, of the circulation of ideas and of people, might produce an antithesis. But it's nothing to look forward to.

In addition, multiculturalism is that which forms a culture. There is no culture that is the outcome of a single cultural element. If it were founded on a single way of life, culture would shackle rather than offer itself as a milieu. Multiculturalism is what made America, Europe, and the Roman's strength, to use only a few examples of a continental scale. Caracalla, with his edict that conferred roman citizenship in 212 to all of the empire's inhabitants, illustrates well the power of universalism, which transcends all cultures in its wake.

Even France is a mosaic of diverse cultures. The kings of France would say "our peoples;" we had to wait for the French Revolution and the administrative frenzy of the Republic to ascribe ourselves the task of destroying regional languages, fight regional idiosyncrasies, and diminish the cultural diversity of this great nation to a collection of regional folklores held in contempt by the political and cultural elite of the capital. Multiculturalism is a notion invented by modern political powers to characterize a return to diversity that nation-states have worked furiously to diminish, control, and even destroy.

Today, we are witnessing a similar dialectic: a world culture that is in many ways unifying, but that also mutilates regional particularisms which lay claim to a certain originality, even if it means tossing the baby of world peace out with the bathwater of globalization. And at the heart of it all, we find ambivalent views on multiculturalism, which, on the one hand, looking at McDonald's, finds that all cultures will one day eat *junk food*, and on the other, finds Astérix playing himself against Mickey Mouse.

Yet, we must consider things in more detail. Global culture is not just about Disney and Coke. With rap, raï, jazz, rock, etc., music already forms a part of this universal culture. It illustrates well, as a matter of fact, mutual contributions in this great symbiosis: the music of American blacks—jazz—first developed in the cellars of Saint-Germain-des-Prés, returned to inspire American Rock'n'Roll. Take, too, the example of the global journey African rhythms made, that of the recent odyssey of so-called 'electronic' music. What is most exciting about culture is that there are many different ones, and that each one can benefit from the other, from that which it is not.

What is happening in Europe today on that subject is puzzling. Europe remains an enigma we must solve. Is Europe merely a geographical state or is it our future too? If it's our future, then it is a culturally-centered future because Europe has this particularity of having had a long cultural history. From Greece, Rome, Christianism, the Middle Ages, the Renaissance, to the Enlightenment and the radicalism of the twentieth century, Europe has allowed, over the centuries, an accumulation of diversity in culture. For indeed, despite the fact that we are all European, there are still many differences between Sweden and Greece, Germany and Spain, and all of this creates a uniquely rich cultural mosaic.

In my opinion, if we Europeans want to play a role in the world, it should have something to do with the juxtaposition and diversity of cultures present here. The other country that could have a similar role, which is neither China nor India, is, of course, the United States, which was built by the Europeans after they savagely eliminated the Indians. It is perhaps thanks to this cultural diversity we have in common that the relationship between Europe and the United States is special.

Our relationship toward immigration is at the heart of current issues in each of our respective societies. In France, the situation has progressively deteriorated. For a few years, I was the president of the Office National pour la Promotion des Cultures Immigrées[92] (ONPCI). The point was to show France its good fortune in having Portuguese, Italians, Spaniards, Moroccans, Tunisians, Senegalese, and so many others within its borders, each of whom brings with them their own cultural distinctiveness.

---

[92]   This organization, which translates literally to the National Office for the Promotion of Immigrated Culture, was integrated, in 1977, with the Centre d'Études et de Documentation sur l'Immigration (CEDIM), which itself translates literally to the Center for Study and Documentation on Immigration, to create the Information Culture et Immigration (ICEI) organization. Today, all of these organizations have been dismantled and the funds have gone toward a museum focused on the history of immigration.

The idea was to avoid, at all costs, their "deculturaliza-tion" and transformation into "regular Frenchmen," which actually doesn't mean a thing, unless you believe the clichés of the beret-baguette-wine bottle. Because being French is, above all, a state of mind, rather than an accretion of cultural references. With my colleague, Yvon Gougenheim, we'd try to imbibe the Italians with the Spanish or Vietnamese cul-tures that exist in France, and the Vietnamese with the Portu-guese or Arab cultures found in this country. We attempted to make a mix, to create an interconnection of different sen-sibilities, which, in the end, improves our French culture. This was a most stimulating and enriching effort. I learned a lot, both about the possibility and the difficulties inherent in the multitude of those heritages.

It is hard enough to extirpate someone who lives in France out of the bond that unites French culture and their culture of origin. If we then try to get them to enjoy a little Turkish or Portuguese influence, it's even harder. But every time work by a Senegalese, for instance, can be shown to speak to not only the prevailing French mind, but also to Italian, Spanish, or Turkish immigrants, the work suddenly becomes universal and enriches everyone.

We must be able to rejoice in the fact that cultures coexist and interpenetrate each other in such a way, and maintain a reciprocated respect for their uniqueness—Régis Debray would speak instead of their 'territory,' their 'borders'—to ensure that that which is exclusively theirs does not get lost.

It may seem an obvious fact, but cultural diversity is the key to tensions of national identity. Willy Brandt said, quite rightly, that cultural budget cuts pave the way to the world's barbarization. Clinton did even better—it was whispered to me during one of his State of the Union speeches—by affirming that education and culture were matters of national security. But then again, all he needed to do was pick up where Abraham Lincoln left off.

Yet, I have the feeling that, in Europe, as in the United States, we prefer instead to place our resources into military expeditions and budgets. It seems to me like we would earn more by funding an ambitious agenda of propagation of knowledge, books, and literacy in the countries where we believe we have key interests, such as the Arab world, Africa, and so many more.

Beyond identities:
returning the world to man

Is culture the answer to tensions regarding national identity? It seems an almost obvious fact and yet... An increasing number of us are calling for educational reform—everywhere, not only in France. This reform should, of course, center its objectives on the importance of human dignity, on the importance of respect for others, the importance of *joie de vivre*, play, and poetry. In addition, civics is tied to a desire for social advancement—not only a community focused on public action or the law, but also a community that wants to advance together.

In the past, this role was more or less fulfilled by the family, but in these modern times we cannot entertain the same relationship to time, and children oftentimes elude their parents. What we are then left with is a succession of teachers trained to distribute knowledge, sometimes even methods, but who don't teach children how to derive meaning out of life. The result is a disoriented and dissipated youth that is no longer able to conceive of its role or place in society, and that lets itself be eaten whole by the mass media and its portrayal of anti-models of individual economic success.

In this endlessly repeating game I mentioned between economic forces, political power, and plain old citizens, educational reform assumes a crucial role. It's thanks to the fact that [education] allows us to move through each stage of this rise in awareness, from outrage to mobilization, that the world no longer needs to belong to governments alone.

And this, *a fortiori*, is at a time when governments themselves must recognize that they are no longer the masters of their own destiny. It is the economic and financial forces that move us forward, rather than the intelligence of individual states. Through the power of outrage and mobilization, a clear and simple message needs to come to light: the world belongs to us—to us, and certainly not to the states, and much less to financial pressures whose plaything they have become.

But people still maintain too-close ties with the state, which feeds conservatism in our societies. Dany Cohn-Bendit made me notice, for example, that public debate, or rather the absence thereof, on the issue of nuclear power in France, or of German military intervention in Libya, demonstrates, even more than the absurdities exchanged on the topic of national identity, the permanence of preconceptions: France is a nuclear state, therefore the French are pronuclear; Germany is a pacific state, therefore the Germans are pacifists.

Can we evade the aporia of unique national identification through global citizenship? I am of those who believe that our prime objective should not necessarily be for us to be proud of our nation state. An increasing number of us now wish instead to be proud of the way in which the actual world works.

Returning to the earth

In way of a conclusion, I would like to briefly return for a minute on the exchange I had with Jean-Claude Carrière. We were talking about this and that aspect of Eastern wisdom, the Chinese belief of the Ying and the Yang and that Greek belief in the balance between different divinities, whose only point in common is our fate and our fervent curiosity. We share the view that this world is absolutely and irreducibly diverse. In that respect, he likes to remind us, Chinese and Indian traditions speak more closely to us: this idea that, for instance, in India, creation and destruction are intimately linked, that there can be no creation without destruction, that there can be no Brahma without Shiva. And yet, there can be no destruction without rebirth, meaning, there can be no Shiva without Vishnu, who does everything in his power to keep the world as it is—efforts that are vain, we all know, for the world seeks to destroy itself and is always reappearing in another form.

This multitude of complex forces, contradictory in appearance, is fascinating and rich in lessons that can help improve the political, economic, and cultural functionings of our contemporary world. It's about permanence of movement in a way. As Samuel Beckett put it, "the essential is to get nowhere"—what a Sufi text actually says in a slightly different way: "As soon as something comes in your way, it is an idol." Intellectually, politically, and artistically, this translates to the idea of never stopping at a certainty. It's calling everything into question, all the time, including what we believe to be the truest, the most just in us. For indeed, this illusion of having found the truth at its best crystallizes us where we are, and, at its worst, leads us to want to impose this truth on others. It's this idea that we are a perpetual flux, of a shape moving toward death, which aspirates all of us; but other forms will follow, forms to which we will have inevitably contributed.

In conclusion, Jean-Claude Carrière made me notice that this dialect between creation and destruction connects to the state of contemporary physics, which teaches us that we are composed of elementary particles and atoms that are all the same. Those atoms are immortal—the death of an atom has never been witnessed—and they recombine in other bodies. When those atoms unite to form molecules and those molecule unite to create a shape, that shape immediately becomes mortal. There is a certain stage at which death appears and dominates us, whatever our matter—mineral, vegetal, animal, or human. The very condition of having a shape involves mortality. All of this is very Eastern. Deep within great Eastern thought we find that the price to pay for being *you* or *me* is death. The price is to be called to die one day. We could have been immortal, but in that case, we wouldn't have existed.

This little treatise on Eastern philosophy reminds me of a Rainer Maria Rilke thought that is dear to me: "We are the bees of the *invisible*. We madly gather the *honey* of the visible, in order to accumulate it in the grand golden hive of the *Invisible.*" In other words, dying is a different way of being than living, but it is still a way of being. The great mosaic made by beings, composed of multiple individuals, humans, animals, houses, countryside, to speak only of the earth, all of that exists somewhere in a greater whole, in a sort of cohesion that will soon come to claim me. We die but are not nonexistent because of it. The being we were was a being that was part of all other beings and that took its place in the immense range of beings. That is a thought in Rilke that pleased me a lot. And seeing my great age, I find it quite appropriate.

As Shakespeare says in *The Tempest,* "The past is a prologue."

The Panther[93]

His vision, from the constantly passing bars,
has grown so weary that it cannot hold anything else.
It seems to him there are a thousand bars;
and behind the bars, no world.

As he paces in cramped circles, over and over,
the movement of his powerful soft strides
is like a ritual dance around a center
in which a mighty will stands paralyzed.

Only at times, the curtain of the pupils lifts, quietly—.
An image enters in,
rushes down through the tensed, arrested muscles,
plunges into the heart and is gone.

[93]   Rilke, Rainer Maria. *The Selected Poetry of Rainer Maria Rilke ; Edited and Translated by Stephen Mitchell ; with an Introduction by Robert Hass.* New York: Vintage, 1984. Print.

Ten

How Will We Get There?

I have been very lucky to live a happy life, to overcome many failures, and to never doubt the importance of my efforts, even when they didn't amount to the desired result. I was greatly aided by certain acquaintances whom I now wish to recognize.

Jacques Robin, lost to us four years ago and author of *Changer d'ère*,[94] led us with the vigor of his pen and voice. The group of ten, for whom he mobilized his fertile intelligence, gave the last years of the twentieth century an intellectual vibrancy still very much intact in theories such as those of Patrick Viveret, who is one of his successors.

That's also where I crossed paths with the most stimulating, the most tireless, the most intellectually generous of friends: Sacha Goldman. He is a man who likes

---

[94]   Robin, Jacques. *Changer* D'*ere*. Paris: Éditions Du Seuil, 1989. Print.

to make connections, to multiply meetings, to ceaselessly tackle new combinations of ideas. He immediately stole my heart.

I began a study with him, which has not yet borne all of its fruit, which looks to answer the world's most urgent needs. It was a progressive, formal inquiry with the most honorable ambitions and the most innovative of means; we looked to invite the most enlightened of minds and leaders, and with the greatest amount of experience, to work together. We wanted to call our collective the *Collège éthique international*. My friend William Van den Heuvel, who sat in on one of our first meetings, forewarned us: *collège* does not work in English. All right, then. We chose to use *collegium* instead, and so it became the *International, Ethical, Scientific and Political Collegium*. Our presidents were Michel Rocard and Milan Ku an, two statesmen who were no longer in power, but who knew all about the exercise of political power and its limitations. The call that we had drafted had convinced, both thanks to its humility and its ambition, not only approximately thirty past heads of state or government, but also scientists, sociologists, and economists from across the world.

We had to bring them together, physically or "virtually," convince them to buckle down, and had to obtain their collaboration in writing documents of subtle but powerful influence that would look to exert *soft power* on the holders of true power.

Sacha was at the heart of this formidable endeavor, which we have not heard the last of quite yet. I, quite incapable of resisting him and delighted to mingle with men and women for whom I had real affection (Michel Rocard, Mary Robinson, René Passet, and Edgar Morin), joined him in all of his initiatives.

What were we working towards exactly? We were seeking understanding of, in all of their diversity and interdependence, the major issues in this time of crisis; issues which humanity might or might not overcome. Our goal was then to offer ways, to offer up our efforts, brave improvements, prudent restraint, and mobilizing slogans whose power of conviction would assert itself to the one-hundred-and-ninety-three delegates of the member states of the United Nations during their general assembly.

Sacha and I were looking for persuasive writers like Patrick Viveret, writers who were skilled at prompting an open debate out of a few simple and clear phrases.

Our first document, which I have already mentioned, was the "Universal Declaration of Interdependence," drafted with the help of Mireille Delmas-Marty.

If I still live for a few years, I will owe those years to Sacha's relentless encouragement and friendship. I shall dedicate them and all of my insightfulness to the Collegium: to overcoming skepticism, and that "no can do" attitude so many situations seem to thrust us into—when we forget to remember that those situations are merely obstacles to surmount, walls that must be climbed first before being able to move forward.

Another acquaintance, who also feeds my sense of engagement, is Pierre Galand, a Belgian senator and president of that tottering and precious organization, the Centre d'Action Laïque.[95] His initiative, supported by our great Palestinian friend Leïla Chahid and her courageous Israeli partner Nurit Peled-Elhanan, to create a Russell Tribunal on Palestine, immediately mobilized me.

This initiative looks to pick up where the great British humanist Bertrand Russell left off when this public tribunal, created some forty years ago, sought to influence global public opinion and pressure the United States into ending that interminable war in Vietnam.

Pierre Galand summoned us in Brussels three years ago and suggested we gather witnesses and experts on all of the diverse legal abuses that the Palestinian people have seen inflicted upon them—not only by their powerful neighbor, Israel, its colonists and armies, but also by the European Union and Washington, which are both incapable of obtaining a promise from their ally in Tel-Aviv to cease her violation of countless international rules. Galand also held financial, industrial, and commercial firms accountable for entertaining relationships with Israel and the illegal colonies it has multiplied over the past years.

The Russell Tribunal on Palestine was a means for me to project my noble ideas onto the cruel reality that is with the assistance of many hundred women and men who are prepared to become engaged.

The first session of the Tribunal took place in Barcelona in March of last year. The second took place in London in

---

[95]   The Centre d'Action Laïque is a Belgian organization that promotes the separation of church and state

November. Between the two, I made my fifth trip to Gaza with my wife and the leaders of La Voix de l'Enfant.[96] Around the same time, Robert Goldstone caved under the pressure of his Jewish friends and apologized for a report whose validity we could nevertheless confirm on site.

We were preparing for our third session that following November at the Cape with a team of South Africans, who know what apartheid is and can help us contrast it to—without ignoring the differences of course—the fate of the inhabitants in the occupied territories. I then traveled to the Cape and to New York where an American version of *Time for Outrage* was about to be released.

I don't think I completely lack modesty. Honestly, what I think I suffer from instead is seeing too many good ideas come my way and being exchanged among enlightened minds, but remaining sterile as human societies continue to deteriorate. And so I feel the need to espouse not only texts, such as this one, but some form of action too. For that reason, I am particularly grateful to my friends who have welcomed me, for more than ten years now, in that establishment that supports civic projects in many of the world's regions: Un Monde Par Tous[97] (as opposed to "*pour* tous"). And this is how I became involved in it:

Toward the end of the 80s, I'd regularly visit Geneva, where I was representing France at the United Nations

---

[96]   French organization looking to promote the rights of children internationally (www.lavoixdelenfant.org)

[97]   French organization that seeks to involve each citizen in the creation of a better world and promotes world peace and respect of human rights; literally translates to "A World *By* All" (which Hessel contrasts to "A World *For* All")

Human Rights Council. It was there that I met François Roux. This lawyer from Montpelier presided over an
institute focused on Human Rights, right in the center
of town. The institute was already very active outside of
France—in Romania and Africa, adding its efforts to those
of international criminal courts. Having identified me
as a survivor of the Franco-German conflict and seeing
my ease at discussing the topic with young people who
were, themselves, currently caught up in conflicts which
urgently needed to be moved past, he asked me to accompany him to Burundi. The Huru president had just been
assassinated—the first step in a series of breathtakingly
horrifying massacres, the worst being the genocide of the
Tutsi in Rwanda.

This mission, to which I happily associated myself, was
financed by a man who, wanting to remain anonymous,
had first remained a mystery, but who quickly became a
true Hermes for me. His name was Patrick Lescure and he
lived in a village at the heart of the Causses in the Lozère
region. A family incident suddenly put him and his brothers
at the head of quite a substantial fortune. Having been a
militant since his teenage years, he chose to make a gift to
a foundation which offered its help and support to human
groups determined to help themselves, but who were
prevented from doing so because of a lack of strong and
brief support. He invited my friend François Roux, as well as
a wise friend of Albert Camus, educator and town planner
Paul Blanquart, to become involved in the foundation, and
invited me too to join the three of them.

This activity, which today provides me with the joy of both "being" and "doing," connected me to more than a hundred projects focused on the defense of human rights, projects that look to support the weak, dissenters, those engaged in educational or ecological tasks; but it also connected me deeply with the Cévennes.

Patrick and François, both seasoned Larzac militants victorious in their opposition to the military[98], regularly took part in the yearly transhumance led by their shepherd friend Bernard Grellier and his wife Nadine. Grellier turned the whole event into a thing of grace: a few friends were invited to follow the slow ascension of the herd along the thousand-year-old stays while exchanging ideas on world affairs. A true poet, Christian Planque, who was raising goats, welcomed Christiane and me into his house above the Vigan, not too far from the mount Aigoual. Those twelve transhumances brought sunshine into our lives and I never hesitated, with each step, to recite a beautiful poem by Rimbaud, Baudelaire, or Apollinaire to my transhumant friends.

Do you see how, instead of creating long periods of respite, perhaps a little time off in the life of this ninety-year-old, circumstances have made it such that my daily life was infused with activities between which I am constantly trying to secure for myself a little reprieve?

---

[98]   Between 1971 and 1981, inhabitants of the Larzac region rose up in defense of their territory against the Camp du Larzac project. This project sought to incorporate land into a military base which would be located in the commune of La Cavalerie in the Aveyron region. The protestors won and the military project was finally abandoned.

The Collegium, the foundation, the Russell Tribunal, and, all of a sudden, *Time for Outrage*! I think that the extreme nature of what it is I seek to accomplish necessitates that I maintain an exulting rhythm of life.

It is, too, what precludes me from being able to develop certain aspects of my personal life more fully. What Christiane represents for me—the joy of sharing with her long moments in which we do not speak to each other, how we simply enjoy being together, touching each other, recognizing each other—I have trouble putting it all into words really…

What my three children, their eight children, my daughter's five grandchildren all mean to me—I cannot even begin to speak of it here. A single phone call from one of them opens up an entire world of emotion and gratitude within me.

I often think that all of those obligations I am currently taking on with such joy and carrying out with such faith will not last much longer. I often think that next year, or the year after that… Well, you know. "That," Christiane says, "I have trouble believing."

And yet, I would be happy to prepare for death. Will it come in the form of suffering? I believe without a doubt. Few are those who, as told by August von Platen, leave this world like Pindar. He is said to have laid his cheek on the lap of his beloved, watching a concert, and when the music died down, his beloved attempted to wake him, but he was already with the Gods.

I already feel quite a bit of my strength consumed, a weakness taking over. I can't really say what stage I'm at; but who cares? We shall see.

Song of the Mum Cupbearer

[...]

Are we wrong to be the notable living
Instead of the battered who would better seize—
Deceased would we hear at last this old song's telling—
Life and its secrets—and our vision be complete?
Among the songs, all of the world's old refrains,
There is one you may come to hear,
One the Wind, the Moon, hum without end—
The inscrutable song of the mum cupbearer.

Christian Planque

A Hessel Reading (and Viewing) List

Adorno, Theodor Wiesengrund. *Negative Dialectics*. Trans. E. B. Ashton. London: Routledge and Kegan Paul, 1973. Print.

Adorno, Theodor W., and E. F. N. Jephcott. *Minima Moralia: Reflections on a Damaged Life*. London: Verso, 2005. Print.

"Agenda 21." *UN News Center*. UN. Web. 15 Mar. 2012. <http://www.un.org/esa/dsd/agenda21/>.

Alphandéry, Claude. *Pour Une Politique Du Logement*. Paris: Editions Du Seuil, 1965. Print. (FRENCH ONLY)

Alphandéry, Claude, and Edgar Morin. *Une Si Vive Résistance: Entretien Avec Claude Alphandéry*. Paris: Rue De L'Echiquier, 2010. Print. (FRENCH ONLY)

Arendt, Hannah. *The Portable Hannah Arendt*. Ed. P. R. Baehr. New York: Penguin, 2003. Print.

Apollinaire, Guillaume. *Alcools: Poems*. Trans. Donald Revell. Hanover: Published by UP of New England [for] Wesleyan UP, 1995. Print.

"The Pretty Redhead" by Guillaume Apollinaire

Apollodorus of Athens. *On the Gods.*

Aristotle. *The Basic Works of Aristotle.* New York: Modern Library, 2001. Print.

Artaud, Antonin. *Antonin Artaud, Selected Writings.* Ed. Susan Sontag. Berkeley: University of California, 1988. Print.

Aubrac, Lucie. *Outwitting the Gestapo.* Lincoln: University of Nebraska, 1993. Print.

"When Death Came to Baghdad," a ninth century Arabian Sufi story in Fudail ibn Ayad's *Hikayat-I-Naqshia*

Baudelaire, Charles. *The Complete Verse.* Trans. Francis Scarfe. London: Anvil Poetry, 2012. Print.

Baudelaire, Charles. *Paris Blues.* Trans. Francis Scarfe. London: Anvil Poetry, 2010. Print.

Benjamin, Walter. *Illuminations, Essays and Reflections.* Comp. Hannah Arendt. London: Random House, 2002. Print.

Benjamin, Walter. *The Origin of German Tragic Drama.* London [u.a.: Verso, 2009. Print.

Benjamin, Walter. *Selected Writings.* Vol. 1-4. Cambridge, MA: Belknap of Harvard UP, 2003-2005. Print.

Bischoff, Ulrich. *Max Ernst, 1891-1976: Beyond Painting.* Köln: Taschen, 2003. Print.

Blaser, Werner. *Werner Sobek: Art of Engineering = Ingenieur-Kunst.* Basel: Birkhäuser, 1999. Print.

Bloch, Ernst. *The Principle of Hope.* Cambridge, MA: MIT, 1986. Print.

Bourgois, 2000. Print. (FRENCH ONLY)

Camus, Albert. *Between Hell and Reason: Essays from the Resistance Newspaper Combat, 1944-1947.* Trans. Gramont Alexandre De. Hanover: Wesleyan UP, 1991. Print.

Camus, Albert. *Camus at Combat: Writing 1944-1947.* Ed. Jacqueline Lévi-Valensi. Trans. Arthur Goldhammer. Princeton, NJ: Princeton UP, 2006. Print.

Camus, Albert. *Neither Victims nor Executioners.* [Chicago]: World Without War Publications, 1972. Print.

Camus, Albert. *Resistance, Rebellion, and Death.* New York: Knopf, 1961. Print.

Cardoso, Fernando Henrique. *The Accidental President of Brazil: A Memoir.* New York: PublicAffairs, 2006. Print.

Cardoso, Fernando Henrique. *Dependency and Development in Latin America.* Berkeley: University of California, 1978. Print.

Carrière, Jean-Claude, and Peter Brook. *The Mahabharata: A Play Based upon the Indian Classic Epic.* New York: Harper & Row, 1987. Print.

Carrière, Jean-Claude and the Dalai Lama. *Violence and Compassion.* New York: Random House, 2001. Print.

Cocteau, Jean. *Professional Secrets: An Autobiography of Jean Cocteau.* Trans. Richard Howard. New York: Farrar, Straus and Giroux, 1970. Print.

Cohn-Bendit, Daniel, and Gabriel Cohn-Bendit. *Obsolete Communism; the Left-Wing Alternative.* New York: McGraw-Hill, 1968. Print.

Comte, Auguste. *The Positive Philosophy of Auguste Comte.* Trans. Harriet Martineau. Cambridge, [U.K.]: Cambridge UP, 2009. Print.

Constitutio Antoniniana (or the "Edict of Caracalla")

Dalai Lama. *Beyond Religion: Ethics for a Whole World.* Boston: Houghton Mifflin Harcourt, 2011. Print.

Dalai Lama. *How to Practice: The Way to a Meaningful Life.* Ed. Jeffrey Hopkins. New York: Atria, 2003. Print.

Debray, Régis. *A Modest Proposal: A Plan for the Golden Years.* Hoboken, NJ: Melville House Pub., 2006. Print.

Debray, Régis. *Critique of Political Reason.* London: Verso, 1981. Print.

Debray, Régis. *God: An Itinerary.* London: Verso, 2004. Print.

Debray, Régis. *Le Moment Fraternité.* Paris: Gallimard, 2009. Print.

Debray, Régis. *Media Manifestos: On the Technological Transmission of Cultural Forms.* London: Verso, 1996. Print.

Debray, Régis. *Praised Be Our Lords: A Political Education.* London: Verso, 2007. Print.

Debray, Régis. *Revolution in the Revolution? Armed Struggle and Political Struggle in Latin America.* New York: MR, 1967. Print.

Debray, Régis. *Transmitting Culture.* New York: Columbia UP, 2000. Print.

Diodorus Siculus. *Library of History.* Vols. 1-12. Loeb Classic Library. 1954. Print.

Doyle, Michael W. *Empires*. Ithaca: Cornell UP, 1986. Print.

Elden, Stuart. *Sloterdijk Now*. Cambridge, UK: Polity, 2012. Print.

Flaubert, Gustave. *Sentimental Education: The Story of a Young Man*. Whitefish: Kessinger, 2008. Print.

Fourier, Charles. *The Theory of the Four Movements*. Ed. Ian Patterson and Jones Gareth. Stedman. Cambridge [England: Cambridge UP, 1996. Print.

Freud, Sigmund. *The Standard Edition of the Complete Psychological Works of Sigmund Freud: Early Psycho-analytic Publications. Vol. 18, 1920-1922, Beyond the Pleasure Principle, Group Psychology and Other Works*. London: Vintage, 2001. Print.

Freund, Gisèle. *Gisèle Freund Photographs*. München: Schirmer Mosel, 2008. Print.

Fukuyama, Francis. *The End of History and the Last Man*. New York: Free, 1992. Print.

Gandhi, Mohandas Karamchand. *An Autobiography: The Story of My Experiments with Truth*. Trans. Mahadev Haribhai Desai. Boston: Beacon, 2003. Print.

Gandhi, Mahatma. *The Essential Gandhi: An Anthology of His Writings on His Life, Work and Ideas.* New York: Vintage, 2002. Print.

Gaulle, Charles De. *The Complete War Memoirs of Charles De Gaulle.* Trans. Richard Howard. New York: Carroll & Graf, 1998. Print.

Gide, André. *Corydon.* Trans. Richard Howard. Urbana: University of Illinois, 2001. Print.

Gorz, André. *Critique of Economic Reason.* London: Verso, 1989. Print.

Gorz, André. *Métamorphoses du travail: critique de la raison économique.* Paris: Gallimard, 2004. Print. (FRENCH ONLY)

Graves, Robert. *The White Goddess: A Historical Grammar of Poetica Myth.* New York: Noonday, 1997. Print.

Groethuysen, Bernhard. *The Bourgeois; Catholicism vs. Capitalism in Eighteenth-century France.* New York: Holt, Rinehart and Winston, 1968. Print.

Guénon, René. *The Reign of Quantity & the Signs of the times.* Trans. Lord Northbourne. Ed. James R. Wetmore. Ghent, NY: Sophia Perennis, 2001. Print.

Hammacher, Abraham Marie. *Jacques Lipchitz*. New York: H.N. Abrams, 1975. Print.

Hegel, Georg Wilhelm Friedrich. *Lectures on the Philosophy of World History: Introduction, Reason in History*. Trans. Johannes Hoffmeister. Cambridge [Cambridgeshire: Cambridge UP, 1980. Print.

Heidegger, Martin. *Parmenides*. Bloomington: Indiana UP, 1998. Print.

Heidegger, Martin. *Basic Writings: From Being and Time (1927) to The Task of Thinking (1964)*. Trans. David Farrell. Krell. New York: Harper Perennial Modern Thought, 2008. Print.

Heraclitus. *Fragments: The Collected Wisdom of Heraclitus*. New York: Penguin, 2003. Print.

Hessel, Franz. *Spazieren in Berlin*. München: Rogner & Bernhard, 1968. Print. (GERMAN and FRENCH ONLY: http://www.pen.org/viewmedia.php/prmMID/509/prmID/313)

Hessel, Stéphane. *Citoyen Sans Frontières: Conversations avec Jean-Michel Helvig*. Paris: Fayard, 2008. Print. (FRENCH ONLY)

Hessel, Stéphane. *Danse avec le siècle*. Paris: Points, 2011. Print. (FRENCH ONLY)

Hessel, Stéphane. *O ma mémoire: La Poésie, ma nécessité*. Paris: Seuil, 2006. Print. (FRENCH ONLY)

Hessel, Stéphane, and Edgar Morin. *The Path to Hope*. New York: Other, 2012. Print.

Hessel, Stéphane. *Time for Outrage!* Trans. Marion Duvert. New York: Twelve, 2011. Print.

"Patmos" by Friedrich Hölderlin & Heidegger, Martin. *The Question concerning Technology and Other Essays*. Ed. William Lovitt. London: Harper Collins, 1982. Print.

Hofmannsthal, Hugo Von. *The Lyrical Poems: Hugo Von Hofmannsthal. Transl. from the German with an Introd. by Charles Wharton Stork*. Trans. Charles W. Stork. New Haven [u.a.: Yale Univ., 1918. Print.

Sloterdijk, Peter. *La Domestication De L'être: Pour Un Éclaircissement De La Clairière*. Paris: Éditions Mille Et Une Nuits, 2000. Print. Note: No English translation of this book is currently available. The original is in German: *Domestikation des Seins: Die Verdeutlichung der Lichtung*. (FRENCH AND GERMAN ONLY)

Hölderlin, Friedrich. *Selected Poems and Fragments.* Trans. Michael Hamburger. Ed. Jeremy D. Adler. London: Penguin, 1998. 25-27. Print.

Hölderlin, Friedrich. *Selected Poems and Fragments.* Trans. Michael Hamburger. Ed. Jeremy D. Adler. London: Penguin, 1998. 11. Print.

Homer. *The Iliad.* Trans. Robert Fagles. New York, N.Y., U.S.A.: Viking, 1990. Print.

Homer. *The Odyssey.* Trans. Robert Fagles. New York: Penguin, 1997. Print.

Horkheimer, Max, and Theodor W. Adorno. *Dialectic of Enlightenment: Philosophical Fragments.* Trans. Noerr Gunzelin. Schmid. Stanford, CA: Stanford UP, 2002. Print.

Husserl, Edmund. *The Essential Husserl: Basic Writings in Transcendental Phenomenology.* Trans. Donn Welton. Bloomington, IN: Indiana UP, 1999. Print.

Huxley, Aldous. *The Perennial Philosophy.* New York: Harper Perennial Modern Classics, 2009. Print.

Jünger, Ernst. *Der Waldgang.* Stuttgart: Klett-Cotta, 2007. Print. (GERMAN ONLY)

Kant, Immanuel. *Anthropology from a Pragmatic Point of View*. Cambridge: Cambridge UP, 2006. Print.

Kant, Immanuel. *Critique of Practical Reason*. Mineola, NY: Dover Publications, 2004. Print.

Kant, Immanuel. *Groundwork of the Metaphysics of Morals: A German-English Edition*. Cambridge: Cambridge UP, 2011. Print.

Kant, Immanuel. *The Metaphysics of Morals*. Cambridge: Cambridge UP, 2000. Print.

Kant, Immanuel. *Religion within the Boundaries of Mere Reason: And Other Writings*. Cambridge: Cambridge UP, 2005. Print.

Kelsen, Hans. *The Law of the United Nations: A Critical Analysis of Its Fundamental Problems : With Supplement*. Union, NJ: Lawbook Exchange, 2000. Print.

Kierkegaard, Søren. *The Essential Kierkegaard*. Trans. Howard V. Hong and Edna H. Hong. Princeton, NJ: Princeton UP, 2000. Print.

King Arthur Tales of the Round Table

Paul Klee's "Angelus Novus" (1920). Israel Museum (Jerusalem).

Klossowski, Pierre. *The Living Currency.* (FRENCH ONLY)

Klossowski, Pierre. *Nietzsche and the Vicious Circle.* Chicago: University of Chicago, 1997. Print.

Kofman, Myron. *Edgar Morin: From Big Brother to Fraternity.* London: Pluto, 1996. Print.

Kogon, Eugen. *The Theory and Practice of Hell: The German Concentration Camps and the System behind Them.* New York: Farrar, Straus and Giroux, 2006. Print.

Kojève, Alexandre. *Outline of a Phenomenology of Right.* Lanham, MD: Rowman & Littlefield, 2007. Print.

"Kyoto Protocol." *Http://unfccc.int.* United Nations Framework Convention on Climate Change. Web. 15 Mar. 2012. <http://unfccc.int/kyoto_protocol/items/2830.php>.

Lawrence of Arabia (film)

Leibniz, Gottfried Wilhelm. *Philosophical Essays.* Indianapolis: Hackett Pub., 1989. Print.

Leiris, Michel. *Aurora.* London: Atlas, 1990. Print.

Leiris, Michel. *Brisées = Broken Branches*. San Francisco: North Point, 1989. Print.

Leiris, Michel. *Manhood: A Journey from Childhood into the Fierce Order of Virility*. New York: Grossman, 1963. Print.

Leiris, Michel. *Mirror of Tauromachy*. London: Atlas, 2007. Print.

Leiris, Michel. *Nights as Day, Days as Night*. Hygiene, CO: Eridanos, 1987. Print.

Leiris, Michel. *Operratics*. København: Green Integer, 2001. Print.

Leiris, Michel. *The Rules of the Game: Scraps*. Trans. Lydia Davis. Baltimore: Johns Hopkins UP, 1997. Print.

Levi-Strauss, Claude. *Myth and Meaning: Cracking the Code of Culture*. New York: Schocken, 1995. Print.

Lévi-Strauss, Claude. *The Savage Mind*. [Chicago]: University of Chicago, 1966. Print.

Lévi-Strauss, Claude. *Tristes tropiques*. New York, N.Y., U.S.A.: Penguin, 1992. Print.

Lévinas, Emmanuel. *Emmanuel Levinas: Basic Philosophical Writings*. Bloomington: Indiana UP, 1996. Print.

Maalouf, Amin. *In the Name of Identity: Violence and the Need to Belong*. New York: Arcade, 2001. Print.

Marcuse, Herbert. *One-dimensional Man: Studies in the Ideology of Advanced Industrial Society*. Boston: Beacon, 1991. Print.

On Jean Moulin:
Marnham, Patrick. *Resistance and Betrayal: The Death and Life of the Greatest Hero of the French Resistance*. New York: Random House, 2000. Print.

Marx, Karl. *A Contribution to the Critique of Political Economy*. New York: International, 1970. Print.

"The Jewish Question" (1844) by Karl Marx

Marx, Karl. *Selected Writings*. Ed. Lawrence Hugh Simon. Indianapolis: Hackett, 1994. Print.

Mauss, Marcel. *The Gift: Forms and Functions of Exchange in Archaic Societies*. New York: Norton, 1967. Print.

Merleau-Ponty, Maurice. *Maurice Merleau-Ponty: Basic Writings*. Trans. Thomas Baldwin. London: Routledge, 2004. Print.
Mitchell, Stephen. *Gilgamesh: A New English Version*. New York: Free, 2004. Print.

Montesquieu's *Spirit of Laws*

Morin, Edgar. *California Journal.* Portland, Or.: Sussex Academic, 2008. Print.

Morin, Edgar. *The Cinema, Or, The Imaginary Man.* Minneapolis: University of Minnesota, 2005. Print.

Morin, Edgar. *Homeland Earth: A Manifesto for the New Millenium.* Cresskill, NJ: Hampton, 1999. Print.

Morin, Edgar. *Introduction à une politique de l'homme.* Paris: Éditions Du Seuil, 1999. Print. (FRENCH ONLY)

Edgar Morin's 5-volume work, La Méthode, has limited availability in English. Only Volume 1 has been translated and it is currently out of print: Morin, Edgar. *Method: Towards a Study of Humankind.* Trans. J.L. Roland Bélanger. Vol. 1. New York U.a.: Lang, 1992. Print.

Morin, Edgar. *La Voie: Pour L'avenir De L'humanité.* Paris: Fayard, 2011. Print. (FRENCH ONLY)

Morin, Edgar. *Le Paradigme perdu: La Nature humaine.* Paris: Éditions Du Seuil, 1979. Print. (FRENCH ONLY)

Morin, Edgar. *L'Homme et la mort.* Paris: Éditions Du Seuil, 1976. Print. (FRENCH ONLY)

Morin, Edgar. *Method: Towards a Study of Humankind.* New York U.a.: Lang, 1992. Print.

Morin, Edgar. *On Complexity.* Cresskill, NJ: Hampton, 2008. Print.

Morin, Edgar. *Pour une politique de civilisation.* Paris: Arléa, 2002. Print. (FRENCH ONLY)

Morin, Edgar. *The Stars.* Minneapolis: University of Minnesota, 2005. Print.

Morin, Edgar. *Seven Complex Lessons in Education for the Future.* Paris: UNESCO, 2001. Print.

Nichols, James H. *Alexandre Kojève: Wisdom at the End of History.* Lanham, MD: Rowman & Littlefield, 2007. Print.

Nietzsche, Friedrich, and Walter Kaufmann. *The Gay Science: With a Prelude in Rhymes and an Appendix of Songs: Translated, with Commentary by Walter Kaufmann.* New York: Random, 1974. Print.

Patton, Laurie L., trans. *The Bhagavad Gita.* London: Penguin, 2008. Print.

Pessoa, Fernando: http://www.sophia.bem-vindo.net/tiki-index.php?page=Pessoa+Caminho+da+Serpente (Esp. 54A-9, par. 1) (PORTUGESE ONLY)

Plato. *Complete Works*. Eds. John M. Cooper and D. S. Hutchinson. Indianapolis, IN: Hackett Pub., 1997. Print.

Plato's *Republic*

Poe, Edgar Allan. *Eureka*. Urbana: University of Illinois, 2004. Print.

Polizzotti, Mark. *Revolution of the Mind: The Life of André Breton*. [s.l.]: Black Widow (Massachusetts), 2010. Print.

Pope Pius IX. *Encyclical Letter Quanta Cura & the Syllabus of Errors : Of the Supreme Pontiff Pius IX: Condemning Current Errors : December 8, 1846*. Kansas City, MO: Angelus, 1998. Print.

Proudhon, P. -J. *Property Is Theft!: A Pierre-Joseph Proudhon Anthology*. Ed. Iain McKay. Edinburgh: AK, 2011. Print.

Proudhon, P. -J. *What Is Property?* Ed. Donald R. Kelley and Bonnie G. Smith. Cambridge [England: Cambridge UP, 1994. Print.

Rabelais, François. *Gargantua and Pantagruel*. Trans. M. A. Screech. London: Penguin, 2006. Print.

Ricoeur, Paul. *Memory, History, Forgetting.* Chicago: University of Chicago, 2004. Print.

Rilke, Rainer Maria. *Ahead of All Parting: The Selected Poetry and Prose of Rainer Maria Rilke.* Trans. Stephen Mitchell. New York: Modern Library, 1995. Print.

"Archaic Torso of Apollo" by Rilke

Rilke, Rainer Maria. *The Duino Elegies.* Trans. Leslie Norris and Alan Frank Keele. Rochester: Camden House, 2008. Print.

Rilke, Rainer Maria. *The Selected Poetry of Rainer Maria Rilke ; Edited and Translated by Stephen Mitchell ; with an Introduction by Robert Hass.* New York: Vintage, 1984. Print.

Rimbaud, Arthur. *Rimbaud: Complete Works, Selected Letters : A Bilingual Edition.* Trans. Wallace Fowlie. Chicago: University of Chicago, 2005. Print.

Robin, Jacques. *Changer D'ere.* Paris: Éditions Du Seuil, 1989. Print.

Robinson, Mary. *A Voice for Human Rights.* Philadelphia, PA: University of Pennsylvania, 2007. Print.

The Social Contract by Rousseau

Rubin, Isaak Il ich. *Essays on Marx's Theory of Value*. Montréal: Black Rose, 1973. Print.

Sartre, Jean-Paul. *Being and Nothingness; an Essay on Phenomenological Ontology*. New York: Philosophical Library, 1956. Print.

Sartre, Jean-Paul. *Existentialism Is A Humanism*. Trans. Carol Macomber. New Haven: Yale UP, 2007. Print.

Sábato, Ernesto. *The Angel of Darkness*. London: Cape, 1992. Print.

"El Universo Abstracto" (essay) by Ernesto Sábato. (SPANISH ONLY)

Sábato, Ernesto. *Hombres Y Engranajes ; Heterodoxia*. Madrid: Alianza Editorial, 2000. Print. (SPANISH ONLY)

Sábato, Ernesto R. *On Heroes and Tombs*. Boston: Godine, 1981. Print.

Sábato, Ernesto. *The Tunnel*. Trans. Margaret Sayers. Peden. New York: Penguin Classics, 2011. Print.

Sábato, Ernesto. *Uno Y El Universo*. Buenos Aires: Seix Barral, 2007. Print. (SPANISH ONLY)

Scharff, Robert C., and Val Dusek. *Philosophy of Technology: The Technological Condition : An Anthology*. Malden, MA: Blackwell, 2003. Print.

Schwartz, Laurent. *A Mathematician Grappling with His Century*. Basel: Birkhäuser, 2001. Print.

Serge, Victor. *Memoirs of a Revolutionary*. Trans. Peter Sedgwick and George Paizis. Ed. Richard Greeman. New York: NYRB Classics, 2011. Print.

Shakespeare, William. *The Complete Works*. Ed. Stanley W. Wells and Gary Taylor. Oxford: Clarendon, 2005. Print.

The Tempest by Shakespeare

Sloterdijk, Peter. *Bubbles: Microspherology*. Cambridge, Mass: Semiotext(e), 2011. Print.

Sloterdijk, Peter. *Critique of Cynical Reason*. Minneapolis, MN: University of Minnesota, 1987. Print.

Sloterdijk, Peter. *Derrida, an Egyptian: On the Problem of the Jewish Pyramid*. Cambridge: Polity, 2009. Print.

Sloterdijk, Peter. *"Du Mußt Dein Leben Ändern": Über Religion, Artistik Und Anthropotechnik*. Frankfurt Am Main: Suhrkamp, 2009. Print. Title translates most literally to "You Must Change Your Life." (FRENCH AND GERMAN ONLY)

Sloterdijk, Peter. *Essai D'intoxication volontaire: Conversation avec Carlos Oliveira.* Paris: Calmann-Lévy, 1999. Print. (FRENCH ONLY)

Sloterdijk, Peter. *God's Zeal: The Battle of the Three Monotheisms.* Cambridge: Polity, 2009. Print.

Sloterdijk, Peter. *La Mobilisation Infinie: Vers Une Critique De La Cinétique Politique.* Paris: C. Bourgois, 2000. Print. (FRENCH ONLY)

Sloterdijk, Peter. *Neither Sun nor Death.* Los Angeles, CA: Semiotext(e), 2011. Print.

Sloterdijk, Peter. *Rage and Time: A Psychopolitical Investigation.* New York: Columbia UP, 2010. Print.

Sloterdijk, Peter. *Terror from the Air.* Trans. Amy Patton and Steve Corcoran. Los Angeles: Semiotext(e), 2009. Print.

Sloterdijk, Peter. *Theory of the Post-war Periods: Observations on Franco-German Relations since 1945.* Wien: Springer, 2009. Print.

Sloterdijk, Peter. *Thinker on Stage: Nietzsche's Materialism.* Minneapolis: University of Minnesota, 1989. Print.

Sloterdijk, Peter. *Tu dois changer ta vie: de l'anthropotechnique.* Paris: Libella-Maren Sell, 2011. Print. (FRENCH ONLY)

Sloterdijk, Peter. *Tu Dois Changer Ta Vie: De L'anthropotechnique.* Paris: Libella-Maren Sell, 2011. Print. (FRENCH ONLY)
More essays, excerpts & interviews listed here: http://sean-sturm.wordpress.com/2010/01/01/sloterdijk-in-english/

Spinoza, Benedictus De, and E. M. Curley. *Ethics.* London: Penguin, 1996. Print.

Thucydides. *On Justice, Power, and Human Nature: Selections from the History of the Peloponnesian War.* Ed. Paul Woodruff. Indianapolis: Hackett, 1993. Print.

Tillion, Germaine. *France and Algeria: Complementary Enemies.* Westport, CT: Greenwood, 1976. Print.

François Truffaut's Jules and Jim. Dir. François Truffaut. Films Du Carosse-Sedif, 1962.

"The Goldstone Report," United Nations
http://www2.ohchr.org/english/bodies/hrcouncil/special-session/9/factfindingmission.htm

Universal Declaration of Human Rights – see addendum

Universal Declaration of Interdependence – see addendum

Valéry, Paul. *Monsieur Teste*. Trans. Jackson Mathews. Princeton, NJ: Princeton UP, 1989. Print.

Vernant, Jean-Pierre. *Myth and Society in Ancient Greece*. London: Methuen, 1980. Print.
.
Vernant, Jean Pierre. *Myth and Thought among the Greeks*. London: Routledge & Kegan Paul, 1983. Print.

Vernant, Jean-Pierre. *Myth and Tragedy in Ancient Greece*. New York: Zone, 1996. Print

Vidal-Naquet, Pierre. *Assassins of Memory: Essays on the Denial of the Holocaust*. New York: Columbia UP, 1992.

Virilio, Paul. *Ground Zero*. London: Verso, 2002. Print.

"Le Mondain" (1736), poem by Voltaire (FRENCH ONLY)

Von Goethe, Johann W. "Faust - A New Complete Downloadable Verse Translation." *Poetry In Translation*. Trans. A. S. Kline. Web. 10 Apr. 2012. http://www.poetry-intranslation.com/klineasfaust.htm

August von Platen's poem "Tristan"

Wolff, Robert Paul., Barrington Moore, and Herbert Marcuse. *A Critique of Pure Tolerance*. Boston: Beacon, 1965. Print.

Xenophon. *Conversation of Socrates*. Eds. Hugh Tredennick and Robin Waterfield. London: Penguin, 2004. Print.

The Universal Declaration of Human Rights

PREAMBLE

Whereas recognition of the inherent dignity and of the equal and inalienable rights of all members of the human family is the foundation of freedom, justice and peace in the world,

Whereas disregard and contempt for human rights have resulted in barbarous acts which have outraged the conscience of mankind, and the advent of a world in which human beings shall enjoy freedom of speech and belief and freedom from fear and want has been proclaimed as the highest aspiration of the common people,

Whereas it is essential, if man is not to be compelled to have recourse, as a last resort, to rebellion against tyranny and oppression, that human rights should be protected by the rule of law,

Whereas it is essential to promote the development of friendly relations between nations,

Whereas the peoples of the United Nations have in the Charter reaffirmed their faith in fundamental human rights, in the dignity and worth of the human person and in the equal rights of men and women and have determined to promote social progress and better standards of life in larger freedom,

Whereas Member States have pledged themselves to achieve, in co-operation with the United Nations, the promotion of universal respect for and observance of human rights and fundamental freedoms,

Whereas a common understanding of these rights and freedoms is of the greatest importance for the full realization of this pledge,

Now, Therefore THE GENERAL ASSEMBLY proclaims THIS UNIVERSAL DECLARATION OF HUMAN RIGHTS as a common standard of achievement for all peoples and all nations, to the end that every individual and every organ of society, keeping this Declaration constantly in mind, shall strive by teaching and education to promote respect for these rights and freedoms and by progressive measures, national and international, to secure their universal and effective recognition and observance, both among the peoples of Member States themselves and among the peoples of territories under their jurisdiction.

Article 1.

- All human beings are born free and equal in dignity and rights. They are endowed with reason and conscience and should act towards one another in a spirit of brotherhood.

Article 2.

- Everyone is entitled to all the rights and freedoms set forth in this Declaration, without distinction of any kind, such as race, colour, sex, language, religion, political or other opinion, national or social origin, property, birth or other status. Furthermore, no distinction shall be made on the basis of the political, jurisdictional or international status of the country or territory to which a person belongs, whether it be independent, trust, non-self-governing or under any other limitation of sovereignty.

Article 3.

- Everyone has the right to life, liberty and security of person.

Article 4.

- No one shall be held in slavery or servitude; slavery and the slave trade shall be prohibited in all their forms.

Article 5.

- No one shall be subjected to torture or to cruel, inhuman or degrading treatment or punishment.

Article 6.

- Everyone has the right to recognition everywhere as a person before the law.

Article 7.

- All are equal before the law and are entitled without any discrimination to equal protection of the law. All are entitled to equal protection against any discrimination in violation of this Declaration and against any incitement to such discrimination.

Article 8.

- Everyone has the right to an effective remedy by the competent national tribunals for acts violating the fundamental rights granted him by the constitution or by law.

Article 9.

- No one shall be subjected to arbitrary arrest, detention or exile.

Article 10.

- Everyone is entitled in full equality to a fair and public hearing by an independent and impartial tribunal, in the determination of his rights and obligations and of any criminal charge against him.

Article 11.

(1.) Everyone charged with a penal offence has the right to be presumed innocent until proved guilty according to law in a public trial at which he has had all the guarantees necessary for his defence.

(2.)   No one shall be held guilty of any penal offence on account of any act or omission which did not constitute a penal offence, under national or international law, at the time when it was committed. Nor shall a heavier penalty be imposed than the one that was applicable at the time the penal offence was committed.

Article 12.

- No one shall be subjected to arbitrary interference with his privacy, family, home or correspondence, nor to attacks upon his honour and reputation. Everyone has the right to the protection of the law against such interference or attacks.

Article 13.

(1.)   Everyone has the right to freedom of movement and residence within the borders of each state.

(2.)   Everyone has the right to leave any country, including his own, and to return to his country.

Article 14.

(1.)   Everyone has the right to seek and to enjoy in other countries asylum from persecution.

(2.)   This right may not be invoked in the case of prosecutions genuinely arising from non-political crimes or from acts contrary to the purposes and principles of the United Nations.

Article 15.

(1.)   Everyone has the right to a nationality.

(2.)   No one shall be arbitrarily deprived of his nationality nor denied the right to change his nationality.

Article 16.

(1.)   Men and women of full age, without any limitation due to race, nationality or religion, have the right to marry and to found a family. They are entitled to equal rights as to marriage, during marriage and at its dissolution.

(2.)   Marriage shall be entered into only with the free and full consent of the intending spouses.

(3.)   The family is the natural and fundamental group unit of society and is entitled to protection by society and the State.

Article 17.

(1.)   Everyone has the right to own property alone as well as in association with others.

(2.)   No one shall be arbitrarily deprived of his property.

Article 18.

• Everyone has the right to freedom of thought, conscience and religion; this right includes freedom to change his religion or belief, and freedom, either alone or in community with others and in public or private, to manifest his religion or belief in teaching, practice, worship and observance.

Article 19.

- Everyone has the right to freedom of opinion and expression; this right includes freedom to hold opinions without interference and to seek, receive and impart information and ideas through any media and regardless of frontiers.

Article 20.

(1.) Everyone has the right to freedom of peaceful assembly and association.

(2.) No one may be compelled to belong to an association.

Article 21.

(1.) Everyone has the right to take part in the government of his country, directly or through freely chosen representatives.

(2.) Everyone has the right of equal access to public service in his country.

(3.) The will of the people shall be the basis of the authority of government; this will shall be expressed in periodic and genuine elections which shall be by universal and equal suffrage and shall be held by secret vote or by equivalent free voting procedures.

Article 22.

- Everyone, as a member of society, has the right to social security and is entitled to realization, through national effort and international co-operation and in accordance with the organization and resources of each State, of the economic, social and cultural rights indispensable for his dignity and the free development of his personality.

Article 23.

(1.)   Everyone has the right to work, to free choice of employment, to just and favourable conditions of work and to protection against unemployment.

(2.)   Everyone, without any discrimination, has the right to equal pay for equal work.

(3.)   Everyone who works has the right to just and favourable remuneration ensuring for himself and his family an existence worthy of human dignity, and supplemented, if necessary, by other means of social protection.

(4.)   Everyone has the right to form and to join trade unions for the protection of his interests.

Article 24.

- Everyone has the right to rest and leisure, including reasonable limitation of working hours and periodic holidays with pay.

Article 25.

(1.) Everyone has the right to a standard of living adequate for the health and well-being of himself and of his family, including food, clothing, housing and medical care and necessary social services, and the right to security in the event of unemployment, sickness, disability, widowhood, old age or other lack of livelihood in circumstances beyond his control.

(2.) Motherhood and childhood are entitled to special care and assistance. All children, whether born in or out of wedlock, shall enjoy the same social protection.

Article 26.

(1.) Everyone has the right to education. Education shall be free, at least in the elementary and fundamental stages. Elementary education shall be compulsory. Technical and professional education shall be made generally available and higher education shall be equally accessible to all on the basis of merit.

(2.) Education shall be directed to the full development of the human personality and to the strengthening of respect for human rights and fundamental freedoms. It shall promote understanding, tolerance and friendship among all nations, racial or religious groups, and shall further the activities of the United Nations for the maintenance of peace.

(3.) Parents have a prior right to choose the kind of education that shall be given to their children.

Article 27.

(1.) Everyone has the right freely to participate in the cultural life of the community, to enjoy the arts and to share in scientific advancement and its benefits.

(2.) Everyone has the right to the protection of the moral and material interests resulting from any scientific, literary or artistic production of which he is the author.

Article 28.

- Everyone is entitled to a social and international order in which the rights and freedoms set forth in this Declaration can be fully realized.

Article 29.

(1.) Everyone has duties to the community in which alone the free and full development of his personality is possible.

(2.) In the exercise of his rights and freedoms, everyone shall be subject only to such limitations as are determined by law solely for the purpose of securing due recognition and respect for the rights and freedoms of others and of meeting the just requirements of morality, public order and the general welfare in a democratic society.

(3.) These rights and freedoms may in no case be exercised contrary to the purposes and principles of the United Nations.

Article 30.

- Nothing in this Declaration may be interpreted as implying for any State, group or person any right to engage in any activity or to perform any act aimed at the destruction of any of the rights and freedoms set forth herein.

The Universal Declaration of Interdependence

"We recognize the integral and interdependent nature of the earth, our home." (Preamble to the Rio Declaration, Earth Summit, 1992)

We the peoples of the United Nations proclaim:

Our respect for and commitment to the values expressed in the United Nations Charter (June 26, 1945) and in the Universal Declaration of Human Rights (December 10, 1948), values reaffirmed at the International Conference of Vienna (August 1993) and fully integrated into the UN Millennium Declaration.

We the peoples recognize that:

Linked inextricably to globalization, interdependence is at once an opportunity and a challenge:

- An opportunity, because global flows of people and labor, economic, scientific and cultural information, capital, and goods testify to the shaping of a community upon which the future of the planet and of humanity depends.
- A challenge, because this interdependence not only unleashes on the planet a globalization of ecological and biotechnological risks, but also creates forces of social marginalization and exclusion (economic, but also social,

scientific, and cultural), and allows for the globalization of crime (from international terrorism to traffic in persons or goods), threatening the security of persons, possessions, indeed the planet itself.

We the peoples consider that:

Globalization tends to favor practices that transcend national boundaries to the profit of transnational networks organized to serve their own specific interests. Such networks function outside of and in contradiction to commonly held values and interests. Globalization demonstrates clearly the current limits of national sovereignty and calls for measures of democratic prevention, regulation and sanctions by means of common policies and common judicial institutions. The time has come to transform involuntary interdependence into a deliberate community of interdependence that chooses its own destiny. The moment has come to look at interdependence not as a set of forces to which we submit, but rather as a project in which we fully engage—simultaneously as individuals, as members of communities and distinct nations, and as citizens of the world. We must recognize our responsibility to act directly, as well as through states and communities so as to identify, defend, and promote the values and common interests of humanity.

We the peoples declare that:

Our common destiny calls for the proclamation of the principle of planetary interdependence.

This principle implies, first, that we recognize the importance of diversity founded upon the spirit of tolerance and pluralism; second, that we set in motion the integrative processes that bring together individuals, institutions, states, and the international community.

The implementation of this principle involves:

- the reaffirmation of the fundamental rights of individuals of the present as well as future generations in a global democratic society that respects public order at both national and supranational levels
- the recognition that the exercise of power on a global scale—whether it be economic, scientific, religious, cultural, or even that of the media—implies the corollary of global responsibility for all the effects of this exercise of power
- the encouragement of sovereign states to recognize the necessity of combining supranational public order with a defense of the common values and interests to which their commitment is indispensable
- the development of institutions representing regional international communities, while at the same time reinforcing both the world community and global civil society—all this with the goal of articulating a common policy for the regulation of global forces, the prevention of global risks, and the suppression of global crime.

San Francisco, June 26 2005, at the Summit celebrating the 60th anniversary of the signature of the UN Charter which came into force on 24 October 1945. Presented to the Secretary General of the United Nations, Kofi Annan, and to the President of UN general Assembly, Jan Eliasson, on October 24 2005, 60th Anniversary of the Organization.

First signatories:

Collegium:

ATLAN Henri, Bio-physicist and philosopher, France

BOLGER James, former Prime Minister of New Zealand

DELMAS-MARTY Mireille, University Law Professor, France

DREIFUSS Ruth, former President of Swiss Confederation

EVANS Gareth, President ICG, former Minister of Foreign Affairs, Australia

FRASER Malcolm, former Prime Minister, Australia, Chairman of the InterAction Council

GOLDMAN Sacha, Secretary-General, International Collegium, France

HALPERIN Morton, Director of U.S. Advocacy, Open Society Institute,USA

HESSEL Stéphane, Ambassador of France

KUCAN Milan, former President of Slovenia

LEVITTE Jean-David, Ambassador of France in USA, Washington DC

MORIN Edgar, Philosopher, France

OULD ABDALLAH Ahmedou, Special Representative of the UN Secretary-General in West Africa, former Minister of Foreign Affairs, Mauritania

PASSET René, Economist, France

RAMOS Fidel, former President of the Philippines

ROBIN Jacques, Philosopher, Founder of 'Transversales', France

ROBINSON Mary, former United Nations High Commissioner for Human Rights,

former President of Ireland

ROCARD Michel, former Prime Minister of France

SAHNOUN Mohamed, Ambassador of Algeria

VAN AGT Andreas, former Prime Minister of the Netherlands

VASSILIOU George, former President of the Republic of Cyprus

VIRILIO Paul, Philosopher, France

VON WEIZSÄCKER Richard, former President of the Federal Republic of Germany

further endorsement:

PASTRANA Andres, former President of Columbia

QUIROGA Jorge, former President of Bolivia

CAMPBELL Kim, former Prime Minister of Canada

MEIDANI Rexhep, Former President of the Republic of Albania

LEE Hong Koo, Former Prime Minister of Korea

Notes